"One of the finest real estate books ever written. Read and succeed."

Tim Ruffin, SIOR, CCIM; Managing Partner,
Colliers International
Reno, Nevada

"Finally, the one book that is complete in its delivery of point by point tools for the real estate investor."

Diana Oaks, Real Estate Investor,
San Francisco, California

"'The Success DNA Guide to Real Estate Investment & Management' is an excellent primer for the novice real estate investor and an outstanding refresher for the real estate veteran. This book should be included on every real estate investor's reading list."

John Utter, Real Estate Investor/
Commercial Mortgage Broker,
Reno, Nevada

The Success DNA Guide to Real Estate Investment & Management

by

Dolf de Roos, Ph.D.
and
Garrett Sutton, Esq.

SUCCESS DNA

A Success DNA Publication

A Success DNA Nonfiction Book

Page design by Trisha Green, Success DNA, Inc.
Cover design by Milan Sperka and Tammy Ackerman, Mesh Creative, Inc.

 SUCCESS DNA is a trademark of Success DNA, Inc.

Dedication

Dolf and Garrett dedicate this book to our wives Renie and Jenny, respectively, for their love, support and encouragement, and as well for their interest in real estate.

Acknowledgements

The authors would like to acknowledge the efforts of Cindie Geddes, John Utter, Megan Hughes, Trisha Green and Tammy Ackerman in making the book a published reality.

Table of Contents

Part I: Investment
Chapter 1
Why Invest in Real Estate

To someone new to real estate, it may seem as though there is a small but devoted group of people who passionately believe that real estate is the best investment out there. And yet when you look at the statistics, only a relatively small proportion of the investing public invests in real estate - most investments are in stocks, bonds, certificates of deposit, and their derivatives such as options and futures contracts.

Why is it that real estate aficionados believe so passionately in their investment vehicle? And if their reasons are at all lucid, why do most people not follow suit? Could it be that many people believe the rules to be too complex and difficult to learn, and if so, what can be done to learn the rules?

This book attempts to answer all three questions. In fact, the first two will be answered right here in this first chapter.

Real estate offers advantages over almost all other investments of such a magnitude that when you understand them, it is difficult to get excited about any investments other than real estate. These advantages can be categorized under five headings:

1. Leverage. When you buy stocks, bonds, certificates of deposit, treasury bills, municipal bonds, antiques, paintings, gold, baseball cards, or most other investments, you have to put up the purchase price in cash. Some sophisticated investors manage to buy stocks on margin, but it only applies to a relatively small number of stocks, a limited percentage of their worth at acquisition, and a limited number of investors. Most stock market investors put up

1

the entire purchase price in cash. This contrasts with real estate, where most buyers "get a mortgage", be it for an owner-occupied home, or an investment property. Consequently a $50,000 lump of cash will buy exactly $50,000 worth of stock for most investors, but easily $500,000 worth of real estate for most investors. The effect of this leverage is that gains (and losses) are magnified through this leverage or gearing.

2. No cash requirement. Related to leverage is the reality that even if the bank only gives you 90% or even 80% of the purchase price in the form of a mortgage, you do not necessarily have to come up with the difference in cash. You may have negotiated a "seller-carry-back" loan (sometimes also called vendor-finance), used equity in another property, arranged a second mortgage or mezzanine finance, effected improvements between signing the contract to buy and closing that increased the value, or implemented any of a number of other techniques to enable you to acquire real estate without having any money.

3. Buy below market value. Most investments have standard market values at any point in time, and efficient markets to buy and sell such investments. Thus, when you live in San Francisco and buy a stock, you pay exactly the same price as anyone else living in Miami, Anchorage, Guam, Tokyo, or Kuala Lumpur who wishes to purchase the same stock. Real estate markets are inherently inefficient, however. Therefore, properties may be sold at their true market values (many are), but many properties are sold at more than market value (the buyers pay too much) and by the same token many properties are sold at way below market value (the buyers get a bargain). In other words, with real estate, you can consistently acquire assets at way below their true market or appraisal values. This is a tremendous opportunity to instantly gain huge amounts of equity for the mere effort of looking around.

4. Improvements. When you buy stocks or bonds, what can you possibly do to increase the value of your investment other than hoping and buying as many as the products and services as the companies produce? With real estate on the other hand, there are countless things you can do to increase the value way beyond the cost of the improvements (See "101 Ways to Massively Increase the Value of your Real Estate without Spending Much Money" by Dolf de Roos, TimeLife Books).

5. Capitalizing on gains. When your stock portfolio, gold, or most other assets double in value, in order to benefit from that increase, you generally have to sell the asset, or if feasible at least a portion of it, and then suffer the Capital Gains Tax consequences. On the other hand, when your real estate doubles in value, you do not have to sell at all. You simply go back to the bank and refinance. This way, you retain the asset which is still going up in value, and which still generates an income indexed for inflation.To the ardent real estate investor, these five advantages (leverage, no cash requirements, buying below market value, ability to effect improve- ments, and not needing to sell) are not merely justification to play the real estate game, but the root cause of their almost evangelical zeal with which they play the game.That brings us to question num- ber two. If real estate really is this good (it is!), then why don't more people actively promote it.

The answer to this question is a little more subtle. You can- not switch on the television and watch a ticker-tape index of how your properties are performing. Some people have negative conno- tations associated with being a landlord. Sometimes people are put off by horror stories told by people who have never owned real estate. Part of it has to be that few financial planners earn money from tipping clients into real estate. In general, the media compare real estate to other investments without taking into account the leverage (let alone the other advantages mentioned above) that can easily be applied to real estate. And most people, even if inspired to go out and look at some real estate, have no idea as to how to eval- uate the property to determine if it is a good investment or not (more on this later). All in all, real estate seems to them to not be worth the perceived risk and hassles.

We firmly believe that the risks associated with investing in

real estate are minimal, and that they can be further reduced by firstly creating the most appropriate entity to own the property, and secondly by following sound, legal and ethical business practices that enable you to reap all the benefits of real estate without having any of the
hassles.

This book is therefore intended as a handbook to help aspiring and seasoned investors make great decisions, avoid pitfalls, get lucid tips, and ultimately realize that while there are rules that need to be followed, the rules are not too onerous, and once mastered, can result in tremendous gains and profits.

Chapter 2
The Experts

In business, as in life, you can't possibly know everything. And in the case of real estate, it's unlikely you will ever know enough to skate by. But you can develop your wealth gene for real estate by reading, as you all know, and by using experts at the right time. From CPAs to lawyers, property managers to plumbers, experts abound to shore up the slack in your knowledge. Never hesitate to ask questions, hire advice and learn what you need to know in order to make a decision. Don't fake it out of fear of looking ignorant. Neither sellers nor potential tenants need ever know what you don't know. And making mistakes always looks more foolish than asking questions.

Partners

In order to share knowledge and risk, you may choose to partner with another investor for the buying, selling and management of your properties. The benefits of such an arrangement can include sharing the financial burden, sharing experience and sharing the time commitment. In today's world of do-it-yourselfers, it is always possible to find someone whose range of skills compliments your own, who is willing to add capital and with whom you can easily work. It may be worth the look.

But before you set out in search of your investment soul mate, keep in mind that there are pitfalls to these relationships. For one, divorcing your investment partner can be even more complicated, time-consuming, expensive and emotionally draining than divorcing your spouse. For another, it is harder to follow your instincts when there's more than just your gut doing the talking. Very few partners will be willing to take the risk or invest time and/or capital without any say in the decision-making process. If you choose a partner, do so as carefully as you might a spouse.

Consultants

Real estate investment requires a complicated set of skills, including accounting, management, architecture, engineering, construction, entrepreneurship, negotiation and sales, legal and brokerage. Most investors don't have all these skills and will need to hire one or more experts to fill in the gaps.

You'll still want to learn everything you can about all facets of the business, however. Even if you hire experts, you'll need to understand enough to evaluate the information given to you by various consultants. Though you will likely employ others to gather and organize information, the decisions should remain all yours (unless you have partners).

Never abdicate your authority in the deal. It's your money on the line, your reputation, your future. Unless the person to whom you're talking has the same at stake, accept their information, listen to their advice, and then make up your own mind. Beware of an expert who tries to make up your mind for you.

There are a variety of ways to find consultants. From the yellow pages to your local chamber of commerce to service organizations to newspapers and other advertisements, there is no shortage of names and companies from which to choose. However, the best way to find the people who will make up your investment team is through personal referrals. Talk to other investors and ask who they used, how it worked out and whether or not they would use that same person for another deal. If you have no referrals, at least ask potential team members for references and then check those references before hiring anyone.

Following are some of the types of consultants you may want to employ. Depending on the project and your own level of comfort and expertise, you may want to consider all, some or no experts at all.

Brokers

There are two primary functions a brokerage firm can perform for you. One is to act as the real estate investment (or raw land) broker when you buy or sell (or exchange) the property, the other is to act as the leasing agent while you manage the property. Look for a firm that offers both types of services. It is always better to work with one person or company familiar with your operation, than it is to try and bring two entities up to speed on your plans, your program and your property. A shared history (if it is a good one) can smooth out a lot of bumps along your road to becoming a rental property investor.

Real estate investment and raw land brokers usually charge a percentage of the sales price, whereas leasing agents take a commission calculated on the particulars of each rental contract. Having a long-term relationship with a brokerage firm or a set of brokers is advantageous. Not only does familiarity with you as an investor, your needs and price range help them to target the right properties and tenants, but your history as a customer can help you get some breaks on their fees or get them to add some services to their basic package.

When purchasing property, even if the other side has already retained a broker, find your own and make sure he or she is representing only your interests. Many brokers are perfectly capable of representing either buyer or seller, but you don't want one that is trying to balance your best interests against those of your opponent. You don't want balance. You want the deal to come out in your favor.

Most leasing brokers will want an exclusive deal with you, in which you promise not to have any other brokers represent your interests. This is fine, but be sure you get some exclusivity in return. Put in your contract that the broker not represent any clients who compete directly with you. Also in the contract, you will want the broker's specific plan of action and associated costs and timelines spelled out. This way, if the proposed plan is not executed you have a way out of your exclusivity agreement.

When it comes time to actually prepare the rental contract, however, get yourself in the game. Meet with tenants and go over the agreement - the rental agreement you prepare, not the standard fill-in-the-blank form the leasing agent might prefer - item by item. You may choose a month-by-month rental agreement or a year-to-year lease or any time variation that suits you and your tenants. Just be sure to include absolutely everything in the contract - even the kitchen sink. The rental contract is a sort of outline of your relationship with tenants. If you leave an item out of the contract, expect it to be a hole in the relationship.

Engineers/Architects/Space Planners/Contractors

Not all investments will require the services of an engineer or architect. However, if you are considering commercial property, a good architect and/or engineer can be invaluable.

An architect and engineer will be needed for the development of new property. From surveying the land to the foundation design to building structure and exterior, you may be looking at an architect, surveyors, civil engineer and structural engineer. You may choose to have the architect coordinate and supervise all the work him or herself (though he or she will still report to you for all decisions) rather than you having to oversee the entire project. This saves you headaches but costs you money.

If you have the time to be more involved, hire the architect and the others individually and take care of management and supervision yourself. This will not only save you money, but will teach you as well, making you more efficient with your time and money for the next project. Then as you get more and more successful in your investment career, you can leave the coordination and supervision in someone else's hands with the sure knowledge that you understand enough to double check the work and adequately analyze the reports given to you by the architect.

If you are looking at making real estate investment and management a career, never pass up the opportunity to do it yourself so that you can learn. But keep your experts nearby to steer you away from serious mistakes.

For a property with an existing building, you will most likely need an engineer, architect or space planner. An engineer comes in handy for renovating or reallocating space for new tenants. If this renovation includes serious building changes, you'll need an architect as well. If you're looking at interior changes that simply change space use, you may only need a good space planner.

Actual construction for your project - where the hammer meets the nail - comes down to the contractor. Whether or not you need a small independent firm or a large experienced one has a lot to do with what you're buying. Raw land with plans for an apartment complex necessitates a lot more manpower and expertise than does a simple renovation of a single-family home. In fact, you may not need more than a tenant improvement company for some jobs. Regardless, you will want a contract. And contracts are negotiable.

It is best to get several bids on your project, as construction firms are highly competitive. Give the companies what they need - preliminary plans and specifications - and ask for a not-to-exceed bid with a fixed fee. Bring the contractor in on the design phase to be sure the project stays within budget.

For tenant improvements, which will be ongoing as needed, get a budget that guarantees costs for a fixed amount of time. You want to know how much it's going to cost to fix a hole in the wall today as well as two years from now. Your contractor or improvement company should be able to guarantee costs for at least two years. Get an itemized list of these costs in writing. Always remember that in business, if it isn't in writing it doesn't really exist.

For existing buildings, you will also want to know what improvements and fixes are required prior to purchase. When you have an inspection performed (and you should always have the property inspected), go with the inspector yourself. Bring in your contractor or improvement company representative so that they can see the property firsthand as well. That way they can be more accurate with cost estimates and you can get an idea of what ongoing maintenance is going to cost you. The experts - construction personnel - may even be able to offer clever ways of reducing your costs while improving maintenance.

Along with your specific performance contract, insist on

errors and omissions insurance and liability insurance. Check out the company's financials to be sure it can handle the professional liability involved with your project. If something goes wrong, you don't want to be left holding the bag.

If you are not willing to retain a transactional attorney, you may want to use the American Institute of Architects forms as a starting point in contract negotiations with the architect. While not ideal (these forms generally favor the architect), this is a frequently used cheaper alternative to hiring a lawyer. Just be sure you amend the standard contract as needed to protect yourself and your project. Get the scope of work as detailed as you possibly can. Specify that changes in the scope must be approved by you, in writing, before they are started. Spell out anticipated expenses, such as number of drawings and progress prints expected.

Property Manager

It is up to you to decide whether or not to hire a property manager. In this choice you need to "know thyself." Some investors will feel that their skill set is incompatible with property management. These investors have a pioneering spirit, whereby they take risks, chart new territory, and set the pace for others. They are the leaders and they know it. They would rather be out finding the next deal than dealing with tenant issues. Other investors are more deliberate and methodical. They don't want to cede control to a management company, which may not have the owners' best interests at heart. These investors are willing to assume the role of property manager. They are willing to be the team builder and mediator, and to make sure the rent gets collected on time, the lights stay on and the inevitable property damage gets fixed.

If you are the pioneering type, a property manager will serve as an intermediary between you and your tenants, allowing you to focus on investing while he or she offers an objective voice for your ideas to the tenants. He or she also adds another line of defense in case of conflict with the tenants. By making tenants have to go to the property manager with disputes, it allows you to stay uninvolved and only intervene when you want to.

If you know you will be using a property manager, bring him or her in on the planning process as early as you can. A good manager is not just an expert at tenant relations, but can also be valuable in the inspection and selection process. His or her experience can save you money when designing a new building by knowing what works and what doesn't for tenants. With existing buildings, the manager can help narrow the field, advising you on what is out there, what options you have, keeping you from jumping at the first set of pretty windows you see.

The manager knows which buildings will take a lot of management effort and which won't. He or she will understand the potential for raising rents or cutting maintenance costs as well as offer advice on tenant selection and retention. Best of all, in order to win the long-term management contract, most property managers will at least consider doing this preliminary leg work for free.

Unlike your contractor, your property manager will be hired under a "best efforts" contract. Therefore, it is imperative you have a mutual cancellation clause in the contract along with specific guidelines of the position. Do you want the manager to collect rent or will it go directly to you? How much do you want in an emergency cash fund to be used by the manager? What monthly reports will be required of the manager? Who pays the bills - you or the manager? Get it all in writing.

Attorney

A good attorney is valuable for every phase of the real estate investment process. From development to acquisition to management to disposal, an attorney can offer the advice that makes the entire process run smoothly. With the amount of paperwork involved in the real estate business, an attorney can legitimately earn his or her money.

Not only will he or she make sure all the i's are dotted and the t's crossed, but he or she will be sure that all documents are legally binding and favor you. There is virtually no such thing as the even deal. All deals favor one party over the other. Which side is favored comes down to the paperwork. And the paperwork comes down to the attorney. So choose yours carefully.

Find an attorney with experience in real estate law and, if possible, one who has successfully structured deals similar to those you are pursuing. But be careful. Many people are intimidated by lawyers and tend to keep quiet, not ask questions or let their attorney make decisions for them. Remember that you are the boss and your attorney is no different from your contractor or your accountant in that they all offer advice but should not be making the decisions. A good attorney will let you make up your own mind while protecting you from mistakes. He or she will provide the legal tools needed for the decision-making process and see that your interests are protected.

While attorneys usually work on an hourly basis, don't hesitate to ask for flat fees for preparation of some of the more standard, definitive contracts. Your attorney knows how long these services take and shouldn't balk at a flat fee agreement for them.

Accountants and Bookkeepers

Most of us think of accountants as the folks who make sure we don't get in trouble with the IRS. In the realm of real estate investment and management this is only part of the accountant's duties. Usually he or she does not do the actual bookkeeping because it is too expensive for them to do it on an hourly basis. Instead, the accountant reviews the bookkeeper's work and uses the information to prepare returns and financials for the IRS and the banks. The CPA (or Certified Public Accountant) will also prepare data for you, the boss. Spreadsheets, tables, graphs - all can aid you in your various decision-making roles. Making an offer on a property, setting rents, raising rents, tracking maintenance, cutting expenses, knowing when or if to sell - all these decisions come with numbers. A good accountant can put these numbers in a meaningful form you can understand and analyze.

But, as always, use your accountant's numbers as the basis for making YOUR decision. Don't let the numbers justify a bias - the accountant's or yours. Numbers should always be as objective as possible.

As mentioned, CPA's generally don't do the bookkeeping (the

day to day tracking of revenue and expenses and preparation of monthly financial to balance sheets) because of the expense involved. Still, this work must be done, either by you or a less expensive bookkeeper. If you don't want to do it - and there are plenty of good reasons not to, starting with the fact that you are most likely going to be too busy to get around to it - hiring a bookkeeper may make sense. Ask your friends who they would use. Or you may want to contact Sierra Financial Center, LLC, a bookkeeping service (in the spirit of full disclosure) part owned by one of the authors. Sierra Financial's web address is www.sierrafi.com and their telephone number is 1-775-782-0804. They'll give you a free estimate on the monthly fees involved. Whatever you do, make certain that you keep up with your bookkeeping. You need accurate financial information at all times to properly manage your real estate.

Contracts

Contracts will vary from consultant to consultant, but, in general, an objective (or conditional) performance agreement (where payment is tied to detailed outcomes) is superior to a best efforts agreement (where payment is tied to the consultant just doing his or her best, rather than actually accomplishing anything). There are still no guarantees, but an objective performance contract allows some leverage regarding compensation if the results fall short of the agreement.

Reduced fees or an increase in the project scope are always possible remedies for the consultant not meeting the performance standards. While the experts are the ones to know what the exact scope or work will be, you can still build in deadlines and demand specificity. Rewards and late fees or reduced payments are an option to have built into the contract as well.

Chapter 3
Choosing the Right Property

Real estate deals are everywhere. In a normal day you probably pass at least a few possible investments just going about your daily routine. Some you may have noticed, some you may not have. But once you start seriously looking, you'll be surprised what is out there.

Once you start viewing the world through an investor's eyes, "For Sale" signs suddenly catch your interest. A "For Rent" sign can lead to a simple phone call to see if the owner of the property might want to sell. A glance at the newspaper shows property for sale by individual owners and real estate agents. Acquaintances might know a friend of a friend with a property to unload. When you embark on your real estate career the problem is not finding the deals, but rather determining which deals are best for you.

Of course you will take price into consideration, but this should never be your only criterion. Don't just focus on bargains. A low price means nothing if you can't manage or sell that property for a profit.

If you are investing in real estate to turn over for a profit, price is hugely important. You will be targeting property that you can sell for more than you paid. But if you are looking at property to rent and manage, the deciding factor may not be the asking price but the terms of the sale. With rental properties, you must constantly guard against negative cash flow (unless you are wealthy and want the tax write off). And that means keeping vacancies to a minimum.

Know Your Goals

Knowledge is power. Knowledge of yourself is an important but often overlooked key to your plan. Do you know yourself? Do you know the level of stress with which you will be comfortable? Do you prefer working with families or businesses? Do you like working 9 to 5? Are you comfortable seeking entrepreneurial help for your investments or are you more of a go-it-alone sort of person? The answers to these questions and others can help you determine where to put your investment energies. Again, don't just look for the lowest price. Go into the investment business with your eyes open. Have a plan.

Planning is a tricky business. A good plan takes into account worst case scenarios, best case scenarios and coping mechanisms. It must at once encompass the passion that lasts for the long haul and the flexibility that allows for change. It means knowing yourself, knowing your finances and knowing your market.

Know your finances. Make a spreadsheet of your bills, your income, and your discretionary income. How much can you realistically afford for a down payment? How much can you realistically afford for mortgage payments? What cushion do you have in the event of vacancies?

You must also know what you want before you go looking for property to buy. If you want to rent single-family units to families, don't buy a bargain-basement home with no yard in a gang-infested neighborhood. If you want to manage a high-end office unit for professionals, don't buy an obsolete concrete building in the industrial section outside town.

It is important to think through all your goals before you even view a property. You want to be sure that emotions don't enter into your choice. You might be tempted by a paint job or a low price or even a property that reminds you of happy times in your life. Leave your personal preferences, biases, greed and nostalgia at the door. This is business.

Once you cover these bases, the next step is to take a swing. Many an investor has been waylaid by the inability to make a decision. If you want to make money in real estate, you will eventually have to make an offer. There's no way of getting around it. So do your research, make your plan, reduce your risk through knowledge and foresight, take a deep breath and dive in. The first offer is always the hardest. With each subsequent offer your fear should decrease as your knowledge increases, but you still have to take this first step.

Types of Investments

Commercial, residential, industrial, single-family homes, multi-tenant apartment complexes, college dorms, small office complexes, business parks, warehouses, industrial parks, single-use businesses, strip malls, community centers, build-to-suit, renovations, speculation - there are more ways to invest in real estate than could possibly be covered in one book. So we'll look at a few of the more common options open to you.

Speculation

There are several ways to speculate on property, including flipping properties. Certain strategies involve taking advantage of a lengthy close or purchasing options to buy to allow the property to increase in value through such events as rezoning or community growth. You can then assign your option or roll over your property to the next investor.

Purchasing options takes forward-thinking and no small amount of luck, but the returns can be significant. So how does it work? It's pretty simple in theory. You make an offer for a parcel of land that you feel pretty sure is in the path of development. You pay for an option and agree to annual payment extensions on that option. This ends up being much less than outright purchase. If you're right on where the growth is heading, you can make big money. If you're wrong, you lose your money and don't even have the land to show for it.

For a less risky venture, you might want to look at a simple long-term investment property. In this scenario, you buy a property and then just hold onto it to enjoy the positive cash flow. When the value increases enough you may consider selling.

Income property can be single-tenant or multi-tenant. The management involved is obviously quite different, so consider which you want to buy as an investment carefully, taking into account your personality and preferences. The tenant's rental contract requirements can run the gamut of full responsibility for all operating expenses (even taxes) to no responsibility for operating costs whatsoever. The former is frequently a single tenant building with a tenant with impeccable credit, while the latter can be either single-tenant or multi-tenant.

Income property can be residential, commercial, industrial or even mixed use. Multi-tenant buildings are more common. The more "multi" the better. More tenants means less risk, even though it also means more management. The goal is to be sure that no one tenant accounts for a significant percentage of your occupancy. If one tenant takes up half your building and decides to leave, you lose half your income. But if one tenant accounts for only five percent of your occupancy, you only lose five percent of your income. The difference between a five percent vacancy and a 50 percent vacancy can be the difference between profit and loss for your property. Once again, it all comes down to the numbers.

Location

There are a variety of criteria to consider when deciding to target an area for investment consideration. Do you want to invest in rental property or property you will sell for a profit? Are you interested in residential or commercial property? Where is demand the highest for that sort of property? If renting, who is your ideal renter? Do you want to live near your rental property (where it is easy to travel for repairs, but where complaint calls are likely to be more frequent) or far.

However, knowing the "what" is only half the battle. You also need to know the "where." When you invest in a property, you invest in an area, a market. So you'd better understand all there is to understand about that market:

* How big is the population?
* What is the area's growth rate?
* What is the area's median income?
* What is the area's education level?
* What are the primary industries?
* Is the market growing or shrinking?
* Where are the high end properties?
* Where are the low end properties?
* Where are the jobs?
* Where are the best shopping and entertainment centers?
* In which direction is the area sprawling?
* Which areas are suffering from high turnover?
* Are new transportation corridors in the offing?
* What are the absorption rates for commercial and residential areas?
* Where is the overall national economy on its gravitational cycle?
* What affect is the current global market having on jobs, land and the overall economy?
* How does the area compare, statistically, to other areas of similar size?

Market information is available from the United States Census Bureau, chambers of commerce, real estate professionals, banks and lenders, tax rolls, industry publications and sellers themselves. If you don't want to gather the information yourself, there are marketing firms all over the country who specialize in such searches. However, as always, let the experts get you the data and then come to your own conclusions. Take their recommendations as just that: recommendations. The decisions are always yours.

Keep in mind that the recommendations you pay for will, by their very nature, be conservative. Consultants tend toward the middle of the road to protect themselves and make themselves attractive to the highest number of clients. For you to succeed in this business, you need to stray from the herd mentality and forge your own way.

Residential

Often the process of choosing a location for your investment is a matter of common sense. But when you are in the middle of learning a new career and when your entire life savings may be at stake, common sense can easily get lost in fear and confusion. Keep your head and keep it simple. Remember, there is no great rush to purchase a property. Avoid dealing with the brokers or partners who would have you believe otherwise. Stay calm and be prudent.

If you are buying single-family or small multi-family units (duplexes, fourplexes and the like) to use as rental properties, you may want to purchase property in areas that will attract the best renters. This means staying away from areas with high turnover and no hope. These areas often look abandoned or nearly so, with dead lawns, high weeds, broken fences and/or windows, and dilapidated vehicles up on blocks at the curb or in the driveway. Property may be cheap but you will attract the type of renter that already occupies the area - transient and probably not interested in the upkeep of your investment. Similarly you will want to avoid areas with a lot of other rental properties. These areas, too, tend to get rundown due to turnover. That said, some adventuresome real estate entrepreneurs have made good money in these types of areas. The key is to know yourself, and what you are willing to deal with on your path to success.

Some investors may or may not want to steer clear of high-end areas with expensive homes and elaborate yards. Homes in good neighborhoods will need to rent for more money to make sense. Inevitably, renters with enough money to make you money will want to buy their own homes. Most high-end home renters will not be long-term tenants for you. Nevertheless, some investors do make money renting expensive homes for one year at a time to executives new to an area. The understanding is that the executive and family will get used to the city and its neighborhoods before deciding where to buy. While this strategy can work, you have to be aware that the supply of executive rentals is much smaller than that of the general population. Assuming you are able to attract that great tenant, there's still the upkeep of that elaborate yard to worry about. Is it your responsibility or theirs? Get it in writing. Curb appeal - what a property looks like from the street - has a lot to do with property value. And you don't want to leave yours in the hands of someone who does not show your pride of ownership in the property, a situation involving most tenants.

One strategy for finding the right rental property is to look in areas that are primarily owner-occupied and have a true neighborhood feel to them. You may find these areas in economically depressed neighborhoods as well as middle class suburbs. Don't let prejudice sway you that poor means no pride and no hope. Look for community pride - nice lawns, fresh paint, clean yards and drives - and there you will find hope. Have your property contribute to that neighborhood feeling and the possibilities of upward mobility.

Hopefully, you will find property that fits in with the existing neighborhood, but whose price is undervalued. This may be due to several factors, some of which may benefit you, some of which may not. If the undervaluation is due to structural damage or environmental issues, it will likely cost more to repair the property than it will be worth as a rental. But if the low price is due to poor management or cosmetic issues, you can fix the problems and still make a profit. Or the low price may be due to a bind in which the seller finds him or herself. Distressed owners are the most motivated sellers.

Ideal renters for single family and small multi-family units are blue-collar, middle-class families. Blue collar (preferably working in a field that lends itself to some ability in home repair - construction, carpentry, plumbing, electrical work) because people who work with their hands are more likely to feel comfortable with the necessary upkeep of the home. Middle class because you want people with dreams of home ownership, but who know they are a few steps from that day. Family because families want a home as a not just a place to live but a place in which life's lessons are learned, which means care in the appearance and maintenance of the property.

Neighbors tend to emulate one another. If the neighborhood

is well-kept, your renters will likely keep your property in similar condition. However, neighbors tend to compare houses as well. If all the houses on the block have garages, yours should too, not only to attract the right kind of renter, but to increase resale value as well.

You should also know what your ideal renter is looking for in a home. Families like modern kitchens, multiple baths, simple usable yards and garages. But they also like good schools, convenient shopping, nearby parks and safe communities. Keep these factors in mind as you scope out investment locations.

Pessimists will likely notice more of the negative attributes of an area, optimists the positive. Make a list of pluses and minuses for an area, so you are sure to analyze it thoroughly. Having this information organized in an easy-to-read format may also help you with renters. This is one of the many areas in which a spreadsheet comes in handy.

Commercial

Demand is a crucial element of commercial real estate investment. Your ability to recognize and/or anticipate demand will take you far in this business. Knowledge of your target area(s) is crucial to your understanding of demand. Do you know where the growing commercial areas are? Do you know in what directions the area is growing? If you don't know the area already, be prepared to do the research needed to get up to speed. Never go into an area blind.

Commercial real estate brokers keep a close eye on the market. And they want you as a client. So let them educate you with all the market information they have gathered. Don't limit yourself to one broker or one firm. Cast your net wide, take in their numbers, make comparisons and make your own conclusions. Never be afraid to double-check these numbers as well. Talk to experts in construction and management. Gather information anywhere and everywhere you can.

Research and Evaluation

A bargain in one city is a rip-off in another. Know your market. Know what property is worth. This means more than asking price. You must know how much other properties in the area are going for. Get familiar with asking prices, closing prices and the all-important difference between the two.

Know how the deals are being struck. What sorts of down payment are expected? How are deals being financed? Are sellers looking for top dollar or a quick exit?

How do you find out this information? One way is to simply ask. Find a real estate agent or broker familiar with the area and put the questions to him or her. Check out the agency's listings to get a feel for the area and its relative value. Ask your banker about the value of a building. Being the ones to approve mortgages, bankers know a lot about the relative value of one property over another.

You can also check publications such as Commercial Record (listing sales figures by town) or go to the local town hall (a veritable feast of information awaits) and check out property transfers for your target area. This is where you will find actual sales prices, listed in land records, rather than asking prices. Remember that there is often a big difference between the two.

Here's where we get down to the science. Anytime you can turn a subject into numbers do so. Purchase price, expenses, income and mortgage payments are all of primary concern in evaluating whether or not a property can be profitable. Always look at these numbers in concert with one another. And try to fit as many aspects of the property into these numerical categories as possible.

A leaky roof is an expense, as is peeling paint and a faulty sprinkler system. Attach numbers to these expenses - either the cost of repair or the possible decrease in rent you can get. Vacancies are an expense. Renters are income. Mortgage payments are constant. Balancing all these factors can mean profit or loss. You should know which it will be before you ever sign any papers.

When it comes to rental property, the key to profit is not found in appreciation or deprecation, but in cash flow. The income operating statement can tell you what you need to know about cash flow. This set of forms breaks down all the expenses and income associated with a property. It is a favorite tool of appraisers and professionals in the real estate business and should be a favorite of yours as well.

A standard form will include the following information:

* Address
* Property description (commercial, residential, multi-family, etc.)
* Size of land area
* Zoning (residential, commercial, industrial)
* Property age
* Building construction material (wood, brick, etc.)
* Rentable units
* Size of rentable units
* Asking price
* Gross rental income
* Gross expenses (broken down into categories such as sewer, water, gas, electric, taxes, maintenance, insurance, advertising, legal, accounting and vacancy. With a commercial property, you will also need to consider janitorial, land scaping, parking lot maintenance and window washing. For both, calculate in reserves for such contingencies as re-leasing, vacancies, unexpected repairs and the like.)
* Gross debt service (mortgage payments)
* Profit or loss

Descriptive information needed for the operating statement can be looked up at the assessor's office in city hall on field cards kept for tax purposes. This information is generally open to the public, so check here first. Additional information can be found in town records at the city hall or county office or even on the Web (check to see which is appropriate for the community you are considering).

Further information (especially the numbers for anticipated expenses) is available from the current owner's Schedule E (attached to the 1040 tax return). Don't be shy about asking to see the seller's forms.

Once you have completed the operating statement, you will be in a position to determine how much you can afford as a down payment and what level of mortgage payments will allow the property to be profitable.

To determine your ideal monthly mortgage payment level, subtract gross expenses from gross income (this number represents yearly profit and/or what you will have available to pay the mortgage) and divide that amount by 12 months. With this figure in hand, you are ready to go to lenders to see how much you can borrow at what interest rate and with what terms. The final step will be to get yourself a mortgage table book or amortization schedule (available online, at your local bank or from a stationery store), which will tell you what the monthly payment will be with the interest rate and terms offered by your bank.

With the asking price in mind and knowing how much you can borrow (subtract the former from the latter), you should now know how much you can put down to break even. Pay more of a down payment and you increase possible profits (by taking down that mortgage); pay less and you are losing money.

If you are looking for distressed properties (and you certainly should), there are footwork analyses and paperwork analyses. Properties become distressed because they are distressing to the owner. Divorce, death, destitution and other major life changes can be distressing, both personally and when it comes to property. But simple factors, such as taxes and property upkeep can also lead to the owner becoming eager to get rid of a property. Sale is better than foreclosure.

The footwork approach to finding distressed property comes down to that most valuable of human talents: common sense. Check out your target area, looking for overgrown yards, broken windows, and basic abandonment. Ask your lawyer and accountant if they know of anyone who might want to unload some property.

The paperwork approach involves public records. City hall has files on abandoned properties (including the current owner) and some even have lists of abandoned sites. Check the rosters for foreclosures and liens. Find out the owner of the abandoned properties you saw on your walkabout. Check the newspaper for legal ads notifying the public of auctions. Check with banks and mortgage companies for foreclosed property. Your state can give you a list of banks and lenders.

Do not confuse distressed property with obsolete property. Inadequate restrooms and elevators; low ceilings; outdated heating, ventilation and air conditioning systems; small, ugly lobbies likely can be fixed, but it will cost you. And if you don't spend the money on the upgrade, you are likely never to make the rent necessary for profitability. However, these cosmetic problems (as compared to structural problems) may also mean the current rents have been lower than competing buildings, so there is ample opportunity for upgrades and the associated rent increases. But don't make the same mistake as the current owner. If you take over the property, budget for ongoing modernization.

Cap Rates

Capitalization rates are used to value an income stream by looking at risk. Figuring out the capitalization value is usually the job of the appraiser, but it's a good idea for you to know how to do it too. With this information you can estimate the difference between the asking price and what you think the property is worth.

Calculating a cap rate involves looking at the building's net operating income (NOI). This number does not include debt service, depreciation or capital expenditures and reflects the building's earning capacity. The cap rate is as follows:

Cap Rate= (NOI/Market Value) x 100

For example, a building with a NOI of $100,000 and a market value of $1 million would have a cap rate of 10%.

Financial professionals tend to see a cap rate of 10 percent as typical in many cities. A cap rate greater than 10 percent means higher than average risk, and less than 10 percent means less than average risk.

Rental Contracts

To evaluate a property and you'll likely spend a lot of time checking out the building and the property. However, with investment property, it's mainly about the rental contracts that determine value. Rental contract income is capitalized to determine value. So it's the value of those rental contracts that can make or break a deal. Be realistic about how much the rents can be raised in order to increase value. A broker's opinion may not be the reality of the market. But what determines the value of a rental contract? It comes down to four primary factors:

1. State of building repair: At this stage in the game - the valuation stage - the building is assumed to be in good repair. If it's not, the rental contract value should or will drop.

2. Type of rental contract: Gross leases are those that mandate the payment of some or all operating expenses (maintenance, insurance, taxes) by the building owner. Net leases mandate all operating expenses be paid by the tenants. Net leases are preferred by landlords.

3. Length of the rental contract: Length must be defined in order to allow for renegotiation and raising of rents, as well a potential upcoming vacancies.

4. Enforceability of the rental contract: A rental contract must have some teeth in it. Enforcement and collection of rent are provided for in the rental contract. These terms and requirements must be detailed and have real-world consequences written in.

There really is no such thing as a standard rental contract. Finding one to work for you can be either a process of study and forethought or trial and error. Guess which one will cost you more in the long run? You should avoid the prepared forms that tend to be too vague and rental contracts so specific that tenants won't sign them. Leasing should be a win-win proposition for both the landlord and tenant. To get a rental contract that allows the landlord some control and profit and still attracts the best tenants is a delicate balance. Do as much research as you can on rental contracts. Check out books, scour the Internet, and ask questions of other landlords. Then sit down with your attorney and property manager (if you are going to have one) and create the best rental contract you possibly can.

Once you have your rental contract you must get to know it inside and out. You shouldn't be looking up answers when tenants come to you with questions and you shouldn't have to refer to a piece of paper to determine whether or not tenants are meeting their obligations. Your familiarity with the rental contract will lend you authority during the rental contract negotiation process with tenants and help you to hold your ground when defending the rules you need to run your building and your business.

When buying an existing, tenanted rental property, you are actually buying the existing rental contracts. These contracts specify your limitations and opportunities in regard to the property's income stream. You should know what rental contract you want to be using with your tenants. Have your attorney compare the existing ones to your ideal. Search for undervalued rental contracts just as you searched for undervalued property. This represents a quick way to increase the income stream and the property's value. Check the existing rental contracts for potential for rental rate increases. The current income amount is used to help determine how much you should pay for a property. The potential for the future is why you invest.

Cataloging rental contracts is another great use for your handy spreadsheet program. List all the rental contracts and the room for increases in any discounts to present market rentals, along with the dates the rental contracts expire. Also, keep on hand a list of all the changes you want to make in the existing rental contracts, so that you can implement those changes when the rental contract is up for renewal. Be sure to explain these changes to the tenant along with the reasons for them - your lender or investors requires them.

In order to evaluate an existing rental contract, you will need to know the tenant's name, e-mail address, phone number and fax number; size of the rental unit; rent (total and by the square foot); date of rental contract expiration; details regarding renewal options; non-standard clauses with the tenant; and dates for increasing the rent.

Inspection

Once you have decided to pursue a parcel of land, you get your attorney to start checking the paperwork. Whether your state uses the title and escrow system or a closing method incorporating an attorney, you will need to know the legal condition of the property. You will be researching the chain of title ownership, environmental conditions (current and historical), possible liens, easements and the like. Some issues can be worked through or around, others will be deal breakers. Be sure to get a preliminary title report, along with any documents to which the report refers. Then go over the paperwork with your attorney.

Realistically, you will never find a perfect property. Most will have some sort of physical problem. Try not to let them become your problems. If they're bad enough walk away. If you can't get the seller to fix everything, you at least need to know about the property's shortcomings so you can fix them yourself or, again, walk away. Talk to the people who really know the building. Maintenance people, contractors working on repairs and tenant improvements, and existing tenants all have an inside track on a building's health. Determine the difference between routine maintenance items and those deferred items that have never been addressed. Routine maintenance will become your responsibility, while, overlooked or neglected items should not, unless you agree to take them on. If you do agree to take on these deferred maintenance items you should negotiate a reduction in price.

Always be sure that the deal is contingent upon your approval of an inspection. The inspection process may be the most important step in your investment endeavor. Never skip it; never cut corners here.

It is probably best for you to hire a professional inspection company, at least until you feel confident in performing thorough inspections yourself. Still, you may request to accompany the person performing the inspection. It's a great way to learn. You can prepare your own inspection checklist and compare it to that of the professional. Rate everything you see from "hands-on" (needs repair) to "hands-off" (good condition).

Some categories to consider are:

> * **Interior by room** (include such categories as walls, cabinets, carpets, sinks, lights, windows and closets for all rooms)
> * **Exterior by room** (include walls, sprinklers, plants, patios, roof and environmental factors)
> * **Major systems** (include foundation, plumbing, sewer, electrical wiring, heating, and cooling)

Also fill out a data sheet that describes the property in detail. Include:

> * Address
> * Purchase price
> * Market value
> * Loans (payment, type, due date)
> * Extra costs (closing, drapes, paint, carpeting, etc.)
> * Number of bedrooms and bathrooms
> * Age of building
> * General (whether or not there and what kind of heating, cooling, ventilating, fencing, flooring, landscaping, parking lot, etc.)
> * Overall condition

The inspection report, even if it is no more than a checklist, can save you money and help in negotiations. The contract price might be lowered, or terms might become more favorable, based on this report.

Inspection companies are listed in the phone book, but as with all other professionals, your best bet is to get referrals. Look for companies who do inspections only, rather than those who offer construction services as well. You want to be sure that your inspection is based on the current condition of the property only, rather than on any potential work the contractor might be able to finagle.

Decisions, Decisions

It's up to you. No matter how many experts you hire, no matter how many mentors you manage to round up, as long as you are putting up the capital, the choice is yours. Therefore, it is of paramount importance that you always have options. Give yourself choices. Start with a consideration of many properties, narrow it down to a few, and start negotiating.

You must always have the courage to walk away. The easiest way to retain that courage is by having multiple options, all of which are borne from logic and research. Don't let fear make you run. Don't let desperation force you into making an offer. No deal is perfect, so listen to your instinct. If you know there is something wrong (that it is not just cold feet), even though you're not sure what it is, walk away. Real estate investment is a science, but it is also an art. And art comes from the gut.

Chapter 4
Types of Ownership

Investing in real estate is substantially different from buying a house. This is a litigious society, and the potential liability associated with being a landlord opens the door to a whole variety of worries. Accidents, discovery of environmental hazards, management mistakes - any of these can mean the loss of your investment. So if you are planning on using your real estate investment as rental property (commercial or residential), think carefully about how you want to set up your ownership. In many ways, "form of ownership" equals "asset protection." When it comes to real estate ownership options, you have five primary choices: individual, general partnership, corporation, limited partnership and limited liability company ("LLC"). Each offers different protections and benefits. You are not going to use the first three forms under any circumstance. You are only going to use a limited partnership or limited liability company to hold real estate. A complete discussion of why is found in Garrett Sutton's "How To Use Limited Liability Companies and Limited Partnerships" (Success DNA 2001). Here is a summary:

Individual Ownership

You bought the property, you own the property, you have all the responsibility and liability for the property and you get all the profits. But will you keep the property, or your other assets, if you are sued? Probably not. So why choose taking title in your own name when:

* You are the sole owner and therefore you are solely responsible for all liability.
* Your personal assets are not protected.
* Poor tax benefits.
* There is a better way to do it, which is not the next way.

General Partnership

You bought the property with another investor and you each own the property and share responsibility and profits (though not necessarily equally.) Sharing is fine but by taking title as general partners you are compounding your exposure. Unlike individual ownership, where only you are personally responsible, with a general partnership you are also personally liable for your partner's mistakes. It is liability times two. Why would anyone hold property this way? They shouldn't.

Remember that partnerships come in two flavors: general and limited. A limited partnership, to be discussed ahead, may work just fine for you. A general partnership does not work well for anyone, except for tenants and their lawyers.

Corporations

You will not hold real estate in a corporation. The tax consequences are severe, especially when compared to more favorable taxation involved with a limited liability company (LLC) or limited partnership (LP).

And while some may note that because an S corporation is taxed like an LLC or LP it can be used to hold title, that strategy is not good. With an LLC or LP you can move property in and out of the entity without tax recognition. Not so with an S corporation. Taking property out of an S corporation is a taxable event. So for maximum flexibility an S corporation is not advised.

Limited Partnerships

A limited partnership is an excellent vehicle for holding real estate, offering efficient tax treatment, asset protection and estate planning opportunities.

The one downside to using an LP is that it requires a general partner to manage its affairs. And the general partner is personally liable for all the LP's activities. So how can you achieve asset protection with the general partner being personally responsible?

By making the general partner be another limited liability entity, such as a corporation or LLC. This, of course, requires the expense of forming another entity, which isn't great when compared to unlimited liability of not forming such a protected entity. Some states are beginning to recognize the limited liability limited partnership or 3LP. The advantage of this new entity is that, like an LLC, everyone is protected, so you don't need to form an extra entity to serve as a general partner.

Limited Liability Company

Like the LP, an LLC is an excellent entity for holding real estate. With flow through taxation (ie. no tax at the entity level, unlike a C corporation) and asset protection features, it is used more and more to hold property.

And unlike an LP where the general partner is personally liable, everyone is protected in an LLC. You don't need to form another entity to protect a general partner as in an LP. Everyone is already within the umbrella of protection in an LLC.

Land Trusts

Land trusts have become more popular in the last ten years. They are touted for their privacy because with title held in the name of the trust and a trustee other than yourself appointed to administer the trust your name is kept off the public record.

But what if you are sued? Does a land trust offer asset protection? No.

When it comes to asset protection, you are much better off using an LLC or LP to hold real estate. Your personal assets are protected. As the beneficiary of a land trust your personal assets are exposed.

If you must use a land trust for privacy purposes be sure to have the beneficial owner be an LLC or LP. With such a structure you can achieve privacy and asset protection.

Again, all of these issues are more fully explained in "How To Use Limited Liability Companies and Limited Partnerships" by Garrett Sutton (Success DNA, 2001) as well as in "Real Estate Loopholes" by Diane Kennedy and Garrett Sutton (Warner Books, 2003).

Chapter 5
Negotiations

You are investing in real estate to make some money. You are looking for property that can turn a profit. But profit doesn't just happen. It is dependent on the interaction of several factors, including:

1. Price
2. Terms
3. Property Health and Quality
4. Property Location
5. Management
6. Economic Market

Property health and quality you will have checked during the inspection process. Property location you will have chosen based on your evaluation of the area. Management will be based on your abilities (your ability to manage the property yourself or your ability to choose the right person to the job for you). The economic market is more of a soothsaying endeavor, but not a blind one. You can't predict the future, but by looking at past trends and studying the economic climate, you don't have to rely on a Magic Eight Ball for answers. That leaves price and terms. Your research and evaluation will dictate your ideal terms. But it is your negotiation skills that will ensure you get them. Keep your head, know your heart and trust your gut. Investing in real estate is a whole body experience.

Know what you want in a deal before you ever meet with a seller. By having your plan clear in your mind, knowing your limits as well as your goal, you will be more prepared to evaluate a deal. Know your own parameters and then don't consider anything outside them, no matter how persuasive the salesman is.

Always be willing to walk away. Remember that the world is filled with real estate deals and there is more than one to fit your plans. Don't rush to grab the first one that comes along without due research and consideration. Considering more than one property at a time (and telling sellers about that fact) keeps you objective. Don't let desperation turn you into a sucker.

Don't negotiate from a point of emotion. Negotiate on a basis of numbers only. Keep your passion for your personal life. This is business.

Never let the seller know you want to buy more than he or she wants to sell. Let the seller carry the burden of selling you the property, rather than you trying to convince the seller to let you buy.

Ideally, you will be negotiating with a motivated seller. Knowing the reason behind that motivation can make or break the negotiating process. You can find out about motivation on the phone before you even see the property. Getting the answer to a few pointed questions can save you the trip of viewing a property you will never buy. Ask about why the seller is looking to get out from under the property; how long he or she has owned the property; when the seller is hoping to close the deal; whether or not (and why or why not) the property is listed with a real estate agent or broker; the relative importance of terms versus price; the minimum amount of cash the seller needs after closing costs and paying off the loan; what the seller plans to do with the sale money. This will help you figure out what drives the seller and therefore how you should proceed with your negotiations. No use spending all your time negotiating price when the terms won't work. No use spending all your time negotiating terms when price is the deal breaker.

Now don't just pick up the phone and jump in with these blunt questions. You'll only put the seller off. Take your time, chat, let the seller get to know you a little so that he or she feels comfortable with you. Have a conversation, not an interrogation. Be yourself and pay attention to what the seller says as well as any subtext that might be coming through. If you can figure out what the seller needs, you can design your offer to meet those needs. Think about it as solving the seller's problems, rather than having a win/lose mentality. This simple change in mindset will change how you filter the information you receive and make you more approachable.

In most cases, you will not make the first offer. Simply ask the seller what his or her best offer is. When he or she answers, don't accept it. Ask him or her to do better. Continue that pattern of asking for a better deal until you feel you've got the lowest offer the seller is willing to make. Then begin the give and take that is the nitty gritty of price negotiations.

Keep in mind that most American negotiations are based on the rule of halves. For example, the seller offers $100,000 and the buyer counters with $50,000; the seller comes back with $75,000, the buyer with $62,500, always meeting in the middle. By negotiating in smaller increments, while the other is still working on the half rule, you come out ahead. The seller offers $100,000 and you think $65,000 is a reasonable price, so you offer $50,000; the seller says $75,000 (meeting you in the middle), expecting you to come back with $62,500. Instead you explain that you meant $50,000 but you might be able to come up to $55,000. Meeting you in the middle again, the seller is now down to $65,000. As negotiations continue, the seller continues to give more ground than you do.

Chapter 6
Purchase Agreements

The purchase agreement is your most valuable tool for decreasing risk in your investment. It is a contract that sets out the timeline and details how the purchase will be conducted, while also specifying which circumstances can mean a price reduction or a cancellation of the agreement. You should brainstorm with your experts (lawyer, broker, property manager, architect, contractor and lender) about any and every contingency that could befall your investment transaction and how long each task will take. The equivalent of the carpenter's rule of "measure twice, cut once," the purchase agreement allows you to look at every aspect of the investment before your money is on the line.

The purchase agreement does not have to be complicated in format. Use bullet lists where you can. Set out who is responsible for each task and how long each will take. Include those tasks to be performed by you or your contractors as well as those to be performed by the seller or his or her contractors. Be sure the order in which you put tasks allows both sides enough time to accomplish each task without the other party having to wait unduly.

Standard purchase agreements generally favor the seller (with an emphasis on the seller's responsibilities and the buyer's rights) because they are made by and for real estate agents. Unless you have your own agent as a buyer know that the real estate agents will be working for the seller. The following are some details to be on the lookout for in the standard agreement:

* Seller holds the escrow: As a buyer you are better served by the clause, "Earnest money will be held in escrow by an escrow agent of title company of the buyer's choosing." You want control of this part of the transaction.

* Provision forbidding assignment of the contract: If you see it, cross it out. When you put your name on the contract as the buyer, include the words "and/or assigns" so you retain your right of assignment. You may want to transfer the contract to an asset holding LLC or to an investment group. Maintain your flexibility.

* Vagueness of new loan contingency: Many contracts include a contingency that the buyer only goes through with the deal if he or she can acquire a loan. This can rope you into loans with ridiculous or high interest rates. Be sure to include a clause stating that you are not required to accept a loan outside certain interest rate, term and point parameters. Get as specific as you can or conversely, make the loan terms be acceptable in its buyer's sole and absolute discretion.

* Incomplete lists of personal property included (or excluded) in the purchase: Some items (such as major appliances) will be left out, others overlooked. Include the clause "any items not specifically excluded, whether affixed to the property or structure or not, will be included in the sale."

* Escrow taxes and insurance held in an impound account by the lender: If you are taking over a loan, you may not see that money for years, but will still need to reimburse the seller (who has been having money placed in the escrow account each month) for these costs at closing. It is better to include a clause stating that the seller agrees to waive these escrows held with the lender.

* Sale includes taking over a loan, but the balance on that loan turns out to be different than what you thought: If the balance is less than you anticipated, you end up having to pay the difference at the closing. Instead, include a clause that sets out, "It the balance on the loan is less than listed in this agreement, the difference will be reflected in a reduced purchase price. If the balance is greater than listed, the difference will be reflected in a reduced cash payment by the buyer."

* **Title or escrow agent choice:** If you are considering creative purchasing (flipping, double-closing or the like), it is in your best interest to have a title or escrow agent who is familiar with such transactions. Real estate agents often have a preferred company with whom they want to work. You want the choice, even if it means paying the full closing costs yourself, if you are going to be creative.

Because the standard agreement tends to favor the seller, you may want to consider printing up your own forms with clauses that favor you, the buyer. Put "Standard Purchase Agreement" at the top of the form, just like the seller's form and present it for negotiation. There's no reason to alert the seller that you prepared the form yourself. The seller will still have ample opportunity to change the form. You may want to write out the agreement yourself and then have your lawyer review it or have your lawyer draft it in the first place. You will want to be intimately familiar with every aspect of the contract so that you can negotiate without having to constantly reexamine. Use plain English (rather than Lawyerese) to avoid any misunderstandings and be prepared to give your reasons for each clause included in the contract.

Examples of the kind of clauses you will want to include in the purchase agreement:

* seller to furnish an inspection report on roof, termites or other hazards common in your area
* warranty of all systems (plumbing, electrical, heating, cooling) and appliances to be in working order at the time of escrow
* warranty of the property being clean and landscaping healthy at time of escrow

* offer subject to appraisal
* buyer has the right to show property to partners, lenders, inspectors, and/or contractors prior to closing
* seller to furnish rental agreements/leases and tenant data
* impound account and insurance to be transferred at no cost to buyer
* buyer may place appropriate signs (for rentals) on the property prior to closing
* details on when utilities are to be transferred, how soon repairs are to be made
* right is reserved for seller to perform walk-through inspection directly prior to closing

Contingencies are escape clauses and they give you final say in the deal. They allow you to back out without losing your deposit. You can have the deal be contingent upon any point to which you are able to get the seller to agree. It can be contingent upon an inspection, your lawyer's approval, your acquiring a loan at a set percentage, the sale of another property, an engineer's report, etc. By having an escape clause, you can tie up the property in order to do your due diligence inspections and review without worrying about another buyer taking you out, and yet maintaining the flexibility to get out if you need to do so.

The agreement should be contingent (at a minimum) upon your review of:

* title report and all documents referenced within: check for any liens or restrictions
* ALTA survey showing property boundaries, existing improvements and easements/restrictions
* topographic map for land and as-built survey with ease ments, utility line and building locations for income property
* contracts existing with third parties others (such as contractors, managers and utility companies) who may be involved with the property: get the seller to indemnify you (in a way that survives the closing) from obligations due to your canceling or inheriting these agreements

* loan documents, especially new ones
* rental contracts
* estoppel certificates: check for problems the seller might
  have with lenders or tenants

The purchase agreement determines your free-look period. You will be allowed time after the agreement is executed and escrow is opened to examine the property and its associated mountain of paperwork for all those contingencies you and your experts discussed.

The agreement sets out how much time the seller has to furnish you with all the requested documentation and how much time you have for inspection. There will also be timelines for the seller to remedy any problems you find. The whole contingency period can last anywhere from 15 days to three months. When the time runs out you have to either walk away or make good on your offer.

Chapter 7
Money Matters

Hopefully at this point you know which property you want to buy and how much you can afford to pay for it. You know how the property will be used by you, taking into account its value and potential. You've taken into account price, expenses, interest rates, loan term, potential income and needed reserves. You have a veritable mound of paperwork backing up all your assumptions of profit or loss. Now you go for financing. Just don't forget all those little (and not so little) costs inherent in purchasing real estate. There are research costs, consultant fees (including your attorney and accountant), renovations and deferred maintenance, all above and beyond financing costs and the purchase price.

Financing

When you hear financing, you probably think banks. However, there is a huge variety of sources for real estate financing and not all will be right for you. Some sources to consider are:

* **Commercial banks:** state or federally chartered institutions of deposit. The number of permanent loans is significant but limited to protect liquidity. Construction loans are more common due to the higher rate of return and faster turn around.

* **Community housing authorities:** established by cities to finance construction of low to medium income housing through sales of tax exempt bonds.

* **Individuals:** Sellers occasionally take back a purchase money mortgage.

* **Life insurance companies:** Although restricted by insurance law, insurance companies invest heavily in commercial and multi-tenant residential mortgages.

* **Mortgage banking companies:** Useful institutions involved in 1) originating loans for sale to institutional investors and then servicing that loan for the investor and 2) getting commercial borrowers, construction lenders and permanent lenders together. A mortgage banking company may even finance the project for the time between final construction and permanent financing. Check out www.successdna.com for nationwide mortgage banking sources.

* **Mutual savings banks:** state or federally chartered, found primarily in the northeastern portion of the country and specializing in acquiring permanent residential mortgages from other lenders.

* **Pension funds:** large money lenders focusing mostly on permanent commercial mortgages and mortgage-backed securities.

* **Real estate investment trusts (REITs):** Public partnerships with a managing partner and many investors, designed to give the general public the chance to invest in diverse real estate investments with tax benefits. Most specialize in particular property types, but offer geographical diversity.

* **Savings and loan associations:** state or federally chartered institutions, specializing in home financing. Both construction and permanent loans account for a large portion of savings and loan investments.

* **State development agencies:** created by state legislatures to address the problems of intrastate low to medium income housing construction. May raise money through issuance of tax exempt bonds.

* **Syndications:** groups of individual investors.

While commercial banks, savings and loan associations, mutual savings banks, life insurance companies, pension funds, real estate investment trusts and mortgage banking companies remain the most significant sources of funds for real estate investments, don't overlook other opportunities that may work for you. Some will consider bringing several individuals together as investors to purchase real estate. Be very careful with this strategy. Technically, when you encourage investors to buy into a real estate investment LLC or LP you are selling a security. The rules for selling securities are very strict. The consequences for improperly selling securities are very dramatic, and include, civil and criminal penalties. Consider reading "How Your Company Can Raise Money To Grow And Go Public" (Success DNA, 2002) to get a good understanding of this area. Also consider having your attorney assist you in this very technical area of the law.

The Loan

You can't get a loan unless you apply, so of course the application is the first part of the process. And you can't apply unless you know which loan you should apply for. The variety of loan types can be overwhelming, so you may want to talk over your options with your experts. But the short of it is that development projects require two loans, a construction loan for building the project and a permanent loan to take out the construction loan. When you purchase an existing building you only need a permanent loan. A construction loan is an interest-only, interim loan with payback due within about 12 to 36 months. A permanent loan is a fully amortizing loan (whereby principal and interest are paid down to zero) lasting 10 to 30 years. Both are available for anywhere from 75% to 90% of the value of the project, so in many cases, expect on putting some money down.

The loan process consists of the borrower sending the lender an application and the lender either refusing or accepting the terms and offering a commitment based on the amount of risk involved. The lender uses the application to evaluate the borrower's financial status in regard to his or her ability to pay back the loan and the investment's worth in regard to its ability to recover the mortgage debt if foreclosed upon and sold.

The loan application, not surprisingly, is detailed and often complicated. You may want to have your attorney review it. The application will include sections on the loan request specifications, project plans, borrower financial statements, project financial projections and current and projected leasing information. You will want to be absolutely truthful in filling out the application. Misrepresentation has affects on a loan application and is a felony.

A letter addressed to the lender will be included to outline information such as project legal description, application deadline, borrower's legal identity and name, project reference and file number, proposed security, application data sheet, proposed loan guarantees, conditions and terms, proposed application fee, commitment fee, pre-closing conditions, broker's roles, broker's fees, costs and responsibilities, proposed closing conditions, lender receipt, borrower representations, date and borrower's (all borrowers) signature.

If the risk level is acceptable, the lender will issue a loan commitment. However, because the commitment contains so much information not found in the application, it generally becomes a counteroffer to make the loan.

Once the commitment is accepted by the borrower, a mortgage loan (a binding contract) is created. But not all are created equal. Mortgage loan contracts can be the subject of litigation. Consider going over yours with your attorney before you sign on the dotted line. A little forethought now can save a lot of legal hassles later.

In states where out-of-court sales constitute most foreclosures, the deed of trust is quite popular. Unlike a mortgage, the deed of trust allows for foreclosure by power of sale if the borrower fails to repay the loan. In these cases, the borrower conveys realty to a trustee who then holds it as security for the loan repayment. In practice, it is basically a mortgage with a power of sale provision. Provisions of law are generally the same for either the deed of trust or the mortgage.

Evidence of the loan is in the form of a note. Unlike so much of the other paperwork, the note is a pretty straightforward document listing (at a minimum) sum of the principal; maker and entity; address of the maker; holder's name and address; interest rate; term; payments; late payments description; late payment charges; default interest rate; a promise to pay; provision for partial payment; provisions for early pay and accelerated pay; deed of trust or mortgage as an exhibit; a section on attorney's fees, governing law, venue; signature of maker and the date.

The note is secured when the loan is recorded in a mortgage or a deed of trust. Either is considered a lien against the property. Recording of these documents alerts the public that the lien exists. In addition, the recording step sets up the priority of this loan (who gets paid first) as well as any subsequent loans.

If the seller has a mortgage on the property already, he or she will likely ask for cash for most of the purchase price so he or she can pay off the loan. The equity (the difference between the loan balance and the purchase price) will go to the seller, or in some cases may be paid by the new buyer over time pursuant to a promissory note.

Know that most lenders will require a personal guarantee. An issue arises when you take title to real estate in a limited liability company or limited partnership. Generally this will be a newly formed entity. Will a lender look only to the entity as the guarantor of the loan? It is not likely. So you will have to sign a personal guarantee.

But some banks do not want an entity taking title, even though they have your personal guarantee. How to handle this issue is discussed in detail in "How To Use Limited Liability Companies and Limited Partnerships" (Success DNA, 2002). The short answer is that you are going to argue that the property needs to be held in an LLC or LP for "estate planning" purposes. If the bank does not accept this very valid reason you may want to consider utilizing another lender.

Both the note and the deed of trust/mortgage will be tough for a layperson to understand. You may want to go over the legalese with your lawyer to make sure the documents match your understanding of the deal. Don't accept the word of the lender that everything in these documents is "standard." Never, never, never sign what you don't thoroughly understand.

Creative Investing

There are a variety of creative plans out there for investing in real estate. Following are a few worth considering:

* **Flipping:** Flipping involves buying real estate that you will turnover immediately for a profit. Obviously the trick is to find undervalued real estate. The flipper can take on several different roles: scout (finding potential deals and selling the information to investors), dealer (finding deals, signing a purchase agreement, closing on the property and then selling it to an investor) and/or retailer (buying property, fixing it up and then selling it). Consult with your CPA as to the tax consequences of such activities.

Double closing: In this scenario, there is no cash outlay for the dealer or the middle man. He or she signs an agreement with an owner to purchase a property, then signs a contract with a buyer who commits to buying the property for more. Next, the owner signs a deed over to the dealer (deposited in escrow) and the dealer signs a deed over to the buyer (deposited in escrow). When the buyer signs the loan documents (to buy the property from the dealer), the closing agent sends the amount of the purchase price to the owner and the remaining money to the dealer. Both deeds are then recorded by the closing agent. Not all title companies will participate in double closings (especially when the owner and buyer are unaware of the complete deal) so be sure to check ahead of time.

* **Assignment of contract:** Similar to the double closing in outcome is the assignment of contract. Basically, for a fee you

assign your rights under the contract to another investor. That investor then deals directly with the owner for closing. If done right you'll get paid whether or not the sale goes through.

* **Targeting assumables**: The key to this tactic is finding loans that have no due-on-sale clause (the clause that allows the lender to call the loan due if the property transfers ownership), primarily VA loans closed before March 1, 1988 and FHA loans closed before December 15, 1989. These loans are completely assumable with no qualifying. Ideally you will find homes in good condition that you can resell right away. If you can, have the house committed to a seller before you even close the deal, so that you never take title and are not responsible for closing costs or monthly payments (another version of the double or simultaneous closing). You assume the loan with little or no down payment then resell the home with a down payment and keep the difference.

All of these tactics are legal, although some have been used illegally by unscrupulous professionals who falsify documents to lure buyers and lenders into spending more than property is worth. They can be complicated and should not be entered into lightly. Do the research so you know all the ins and outs of such deals before you even go looking for an investment. There are plenty of charlatans out there who know how to sucker a rooky investor with creative financing deals that cannot be completed.

You need to know which questions to ask, and which answers to be wary of. For instance, some lenders have implemented title seasoning requirements in which a seller must own the property for 12 months before selling it. This could kill many a creative deal. You must know the requirements of the lender with whom you (or any other party in your deal) are dealing. If you can't get around the seasoning requirement with one lender try finding another lender with no such clause.

There are also quite a few creative tactics you can use when looking at the specifics of financing and structuring the deal. The following hints could prove helpful:

* Consider applying for a loan with adjustable rates. Rates will likely go up over time, but over that time you will have increased the profitability of your investment and adjusted rents to take into account rising rates. In the meantime, you will have been able to get into the property at a lower rate. It's a tradeoff to be sure, but a manageable one worth considering.

* Similar to the adjustable rate loan, get the seller to carry a graduated payment loan. Get in cheap, keep your expenses down and raise the rents to cover the payment increases.

* Have the seller carry an interest-only loan. You won't be paying on the principal and can put the money away or into a more profitable venture. Yes, you will have a balloon payment at the end, but you can plan for that while your money continues to work for you. Sometimes it is actually better to put off until tomorrow what you could do today. Try not to sign a note with a balloon payment due in less than seven years. You will need that time to figure out how to pay off that lump sum or whether you should sell or refinance the property.

* Always have a backdoor clause on your notes. A backdoor clause allows you to extend the loan term (with a penalty) if payoff time comes and you're not ready. This adds some safety to loans with balloon payments.

* If you are considering an existing rental property, have the owner evict any problem tenants before you buy. When you buy rental property you want to take over its assets not its hassles.

* Always give yourself a first right of refusal for sale of the note. This clause allows you to make the first offer on buying the note back from the seller (often at a discount).

* Keep your expenses low by having the seller carry a note with no payments. This also works well with the first right of refusal clause.

Chapter 8
The Closing

The closing is nothing more than the ceremony during which ownership of the company is legally transferred from seller to buyer. The buyer hands over the money, the seller hands over the deed and the keys. The ceremony is relatively painless, but everything leading up to that moment may not be so.

By this point your real estate investment has created its own tower of paperwork. Hopefully all the documents are accurate and have been thoroughly checked because there's no turning back after the closing.

The closing is usually performed in the offices of an attorney or an escrow company.

Paperwork

The buyer's stack of paperwork is smaller than the sellers. As the buyer, you have the purchase agreement, the loan application (or loan assumption application), approvals you must grant in writing and the closing document.

The seller's paperwork will include the rental contracts, original loan documents, warranties and representations, complete accounting, contract copies, maintenance agreements, estoppel agreements, general warranty deed, formal assignment of rental contracts and contracts for the closing.

Third party paperwork will include preliminary title commitment, title insurance policy, loan documents (originated by lender) and possibly (and recommended) acknowledgement by tenants of assignment of rental contracts.

Buyer Responsibilities

As the buyer, you've done most of your work already. You originated the purchase agreement and you've approved all the paperwork (or you wouldn't have offered the purchase agreement) and you're ready to pay with your financing in place. You'd better hope your evaluation of the property is accurate.

Seller Responsibilities

Estoppel agreements: One of the most time-consuming closure requirements for the seller is the estoppel agreement. This document states that the rental contract is in force, the tenant is in possession of the premises, is paying rent and that neither the tenant nor the landlord is in default. It will also detail the amount of rent being paid and the deposit amount being held. The hassle is not due to the document - it's really pretty simple - but in getting the tenants to sign them. Tenants are not usually eager to help the landlord sell the property and bring in a new landlord who will almost certainly raise the rent. But whether or not the landlord can get the estoppel agreements easily, lender and buyers insist upon them for loans or sales.

Deposits: Rental contract deposits need to be transferred to the buyer, and utility deposits need to be transferred or used to adjust the purchase price.

Warranties and assignments: Simple and specific language should be used to assign the rental contracts and warranties. As long as the document assignments pass approval by the appropriate third parties the assignments may be perfected.

It is important to note that there is a great deal of documentation associated with real estate transactions. It is your responsibility, and right, to review them all and approve of them or, if it is

appropriate, disapprove of them. There is not much room for negotiation after they have been signed.

Chapter 9
Taxes and Recordkeeping

Tax laws are changing so fast in our modern era that it has become almost impossible for the layperson to keep up. Even tax professionals are working at a sprint to ensure their knowledge meets customer needs. Yet tax implications cannot be ignored when considering a real estate deal. In fact, it is often tax law that dictates the structure of the deal. You will want to consider how much you are making now and expect to make in the future, and how you want to use the property and for how long, before you contact a tax professional on how to treat the property for tax purposes.

An excellent discussion of tax strategies for real estate investments can be found in "Real Estate Loopholes" by Diane Kennedy and Garrett Sutton (Warner Books, 2003).

A complete discussion of taxation is too involved for an overview book of this nature so we will deal with only a few points here.

Depreciation is always a point of interest for real estate owners. It is based on the government's assumption that residential buildings tend to wear out over a 27 ½ year period (39 years for commercial or industrial properties). Please note that the government's period for depreciation may change. That said, a building owner is allowed to divide the cost of a building by the number of government-declared useful life years and take that number as a depreciation allowance. Note that it is just the building that is depreciated. The land, of course, isn't going anywhere and its useful life isn't depreciated. Furthermore, personal property items, such as carpets, stoves, dishwashers and range hoods, can be depreciated over much shorter terms. This means more depreciation expense per year.

The depreciation schedule is determined on the basis of purchase price plus capital improvement costs. Other costs are considered operating or partnership expenses and, for taxes, are expensed during the current year.

Recapture comes into play when the property is sold for more than the depreciated value. At that point the depreciation expense that is recaptured is subject to either ordinary or capital gains tax rate, depending on the type of depreciation schedule originally used. If you sold a property that you had depreciated by $100,000 the first $100,000 in profit gets recaptured at these usually higher rates.

After recapture is calculated then comes capital gains. The balance of this profit above and beyond the original recaptured basis of the property is the capital gain, which is usually taxed at lower rates, 15% under the new act if the property has been held for one year. Congress may change this rate once again so be aware of what the future may hold. The new buyer starts over with their basis being what is paid for the property. Profits are future considerations.

It is important to know that only income-producing buildings (not land) are eligible for depreciation. The building must be rented for housing or business uses. You can't depreciate your personal residence.

There are several areas to consider when planning for taxes, and which can help in your initial decision-making process when choosing an investment. One is the land-to-improvement ratio. This little piece of math can tell you how much tax you might be able to write off on a building. First you find the going price for land sales for the last year or so (check with a title company or the county recorder's office for the info), then find the going price for houses for that same period. Subtract the former from the latter and you have a ballpark figure for improvements in the area (the buildings). Remember, the improvements may be depreciated.

No matter how you decide to improve the property and no matter how you decide to value such improvements, always be absolutely sure that you can back up your figures in case of audit. Keep your accountant and attorney in the loop on any tax issues. The IRS is not an institution you ever want to face alone or unprepared.

Unlike improvements (which must be capitalized and depreciated), repairs are deducted the year they are made, making them more valuable for tax purposes. So what's the difference between remodeling the bathroom and repairing the bathroom? Maybe nothing but the notations you make on the back of receipts and bills. Certainly, making notations is a good habit to acquire.

So who should make these repairs and do the remodeling? Your first instinct is probably to do it yourself. Well, maybe not. If you do your own labor, you do cut your costs. But you cannot deduct your own labor on your taxes. Hire someone else and it's deductible as a business expense. Keep good records, however, so these independent contractors are not confused with employees (making you responsible for withholding tax, state and local payroll taxes and Social Security taxes). Hire contractors by the job rather than on a salary and let them pay their own taxes.

Management is also deductible if done by someone other than yourself. If you decide to perform management duties on your own (even if only part-time as long as you can show your goal of owning the property is to rent it and bring in income), you can, however, deduct office expenses, travel and other expenses strictly related to the running of your rental business. Again, keep good records. The only antidote to audit is good records.

It is important to again to again note that record-keeping and accounting requirements can quickly bury the new real estate investor. In fact, most investors never progress beyond four properties because the paperwork is too overwhelming. Here are some tips to help you keep up with the requirements. This list is not complete. It is used as a guideline to get you started.

There are two types of financial records that you will be required to keep for your real estate investment. First, you will need to keep long-term or permanent records. These records should include the closing documents for the initial purchase of your property as well as documentation for additions and improvements to the property. These items are booked as assets on your balance sheet and remain on your financial statements as long as you own the property. You will also need to keep track of tenant deposits that you still hold. At some point, these deposits will either become income (tenant forfeiture) or will be returned to the tenant. Until then, they are liabilities for your company and are recorded on the company's balance sheet. Keep these records with your permanent files. The permanent files need to be kept until five years after the disposal of the property.

The second group of records relate to the annual income and expense amounts. These records would include the rent receipts from the property and monthly expenses such as mortgage payments, property tax, management fees, repairs and the like. These items are all recorded on your profit and loss statement. You will need to keep these files for five years after the filing of your tax returns.

You don't need to master bookkeeping and accounting to keep orderly records. In fact, you can hire someone to do that bookkeeping for you. But, it is your responsibility to provide accurate information so that you can, in turn, receive accurate and timely financial statements. For more complete information on accounting and financial recordkeeping see the Success DNA's book, "Easy Accounting for Real Estate Investors" by Diane Kennedy, CPA.

Chapter 10
Reselling

Once again (and always) it is important for you to know all your options with regard to your real estate investment. While you may have purchased the property with the intent to use it as a rental property, that is not always the most feasible (or even possible) course of action. Some properties simply aren't profitable, no matter how the paperwork reads. Others may be victims of changing markets, changing neighborhoods or changing tastes. There is no predicting the future in real estate, but knowing your options certainly increases your chance of having a "lucky" outcome. Always prepare for your exit, even before you commit to your entrance. Reselling property is not something to learn later, down the line, when you need to "get out now." Reselling should be a consideration to your plan from its very inception.

If a property isn't operating at a rate you want or it turns out simply to be more hassle than it is worth, sell it. And don't be intimidated by the process. Just think how much you know about selling now that you've gone through the buying process. What you haven't figured out you can learn. What you can't learn, you can hire (after all, you know which experts to use now and you have a working relationship with your own stable of them).

Sometimes you will want to sell a property that is doing very well, simply because you have improved it so well, gotten the rental contracts in such perfect order, that the chance for profit outweighs the monthly income and attendant headaches.

If equity has built up in your property and you have good credit (along with good income), refinancing is certainly an option.

Refinance (with an assumable loan) before you sell and you keep the money and not the payments - they become the burden of the buyer. But be sure you keep interest rates low enough to make the sale viable. Then offer to take a low down payment to help entice the buyer into taking over payments.

You may want to keep the property you have worked so hard to acquire. It may be the beginning of your real estate empire. Empire building takes capital. Refinancing existing properties can be a good way to get that needed capital.

Let's not forget your constant companion - taxes. There are so many tax benefits to real estate that although your pre tax returns may be modest your after tax returns may be spectacular.

You might also consider an exchange, where you sell the property and reinvest in another of the same kind property without paying any taxes. Exchanges are an excellent way to build real estate wealth but they can be complicated, so keep your attorney involved. For more information on tax free real estate exchanges, also known as 1031 or Starker exchanges, see "Real Estate Loopholes" by Diane Kennedy and Garrett Sutton (Warner Books, 2003).

If you decide to pursue a sale of your investment property and you don't need or have a plan for the influx of cash, consider carrying a note. Don't let the possibility of a check with a lot of zeros keep you from fully evaluating your options. Carrying a note may mean a higher price for the property, a quicker sale, a break on your taxes and an ongoing source of income in the form of monthly pay-ments.

You may even want to sell the property to a tenant through a lease option. In this scenario, you get the tax benefits of owning the property and the tenants handle maintenance. But you keep your equity and future appreciations. Set a high option price to account for inflation or designate in the contract that an appraiser will deter-mine such before the sale.

Even if you designate the use of an appraiser, you can charge an option fee anyway. The option to buy a property is a big deal and should be accorded the respect that comes with the laying out of money. Your fee can be small (under $100) or large (several thousand dollars), but it is not refundable. It is also not taxable until the option expires or is exercised - another one of those handy examples of getting the money now and paying the tax later that make real estate such a good investment tool.

However, the flat option fee is not the only way to collect. Lower rent with a high fee and/or high option price may serve as a great incentive during a sluggish economy or in a sluggish market. But be sure to set the option price high enough to account for inflation and appreciation and make it clear to all parties that the option fee is not refundable.

You may also collect increased rent in exchange for the privilege of an option. You may even choose to deduct the increase from the final purchase price, serving as a nice reward for the tenant paying the increased rent and exercising the option. If he or she does not exercise the option, you got a higher rent for the duration of the lease. Not a bad deal either way.

No matter which option you choose, be careful with the wording of the contract so that the fee or increased rent can't be seen as equity in the property. Tenants have been known to try this ploy - and they've won. Make it crystal clear that the option fee or increase in rent being taken from the purchase price is not refundable in any way should the option expire.

Justifying Your Price

When buyers come a-calling they will want to know the history of the building, your plan as it has been implemented, what can be expected for the future (five years is a good range) and the competition.

The history of the property will include all that research you did when buying the building. Remember that tenant and rental contract spreadsheet you did? Inspection reports? Even photos will come in handy. All this history will give a baseline for an analysis of the improvements you have made (in the building as well as in the rental contracts).

The plan you have implemented (showing your initial steps as well as how operations are currently run) is a big bonus to buyers who want to jump into a successful operation. These are the folks looking for tax shelter and/or monthly income. They are not willing to put in the work required to increase the value for resale. They may be willing to pay a little more if your experience and advice is part of the package.

Your rental contracts dictate the potential of the building. How you have managed the rental contracts will account for most (if not all) your profit. The fact that the value is based on a working plan assures the new buyer that he or she can see similar returns without starting from scratch. He or she can just keep on the path you have forged.

It cannot be stressed enough that for a buyer income equates to value. The steadier, larger and more reliable stream of income the greater value the buyer will see in your property.

The proof of all your paperwork, your grand plan and sterling projections, lies in the numbers. Knowing which numbers is important. Talk to your consultants, get their input and advice.

None of this information is for public consumption. Deliver it only to serious buyers, those who have signed a nondisclosure agreement and those that have the ability to buy your property (as opposed to those with the ability to waste your time.)

Sales Package

We're a visual society. Adding visuals to your sales package is easy and more than worth the price and effort. Photos of the building and land are a must, but adding a map showing the building in relation to the surrounding community and transportation corridors adds the sort of information needed by the buyer to make a decision. Aerial photos enhance the buyer's understanding of the area and the property and are worth the price. Multi-tenant properties should also include floor and site plans.

Pictures are nice; they will capture the attention of potential buyers. But it is the numbers that will bring the buyer in for a discussion. Spreadsheets lend themselves well to a sales package as they are easy to interpret and can show a lot of information in a small amount of space. You don't want to include your accounting here, as mentioned above. It's best to talk to your experts about what you can safely disclose, such as vacancy level, gross income, potential income, net operating income, property management fees, net income before debt service, debt service, cash flow, increase or decrease per year (as a percentage), operating expenses, operating expenses retrieved from tenants and operating income.

Compare your building with the market average for other buildings if you have reliable third-party data, but not with individual buildings. Avoid degrading other properties at all costs. Let your property sell itself on its own merits.

Improvements

You may want to make some improvements to the property before you set your price. Just be sure that the improvements will actually make the property more valuable (or at least bring a faster sale) before you start writing checks to the local home improvement store. How do you know if improvements are worth your time and money? A good ratio to remember is 1:1.5 - spending a buck brings a buck and a half in increased value.

In Chapter 3 we discussed how to figure out the value of a piece of property. Use those skills again to see where your property fits in the monetary hierarchy of similar properties in the area. If your property sits at the low end of the hierarchy, improvements might help it jump up a few pegs. But if the property is already sitting pretty, improvements won't do much, if anything, but price it out of the market.

Some standard improvements to consider (if you determine they meet the 1:1.5 guideline) are: painting (inside and out), cleaning up the landscaping and a thorough cleaning of the entire property.

When selling, you will want to prove the condition of the property. Keep logs of maintenance and improvements that can be cross-referenced with the expenses. Combined with the reports established when you bought the building, these logs will be good proof that your building is in fine shape.

Real Estate Agents

You likely know quite a bit about real estate agents from your dealings in buying your property, but it may be a different game from your perspective as a seller. Yes, an agent gets paid, but they don't get the money for just putting up a bunch of "for sale" signs. Real estate agents do not earn their commissions until the property sells. So their best interest is usually the same as yours - a good price or a quick sale (these seldom go hand in hand). You need to be clear, however, which is more important to you - price or speed.

When you employ the expertise of a real estate agent, you will sign a listing agreement. This contract will set out how the agent will be paid. Some use a percentage (set or sliding) of the sale, some a flat fee, and others will receive the difference between a minimum price you set and the actual purchase price.

While some large, complicated commercial and industrial deals may be farmed out to multiple agents, you will usually be asked to sign an exclusive agreement for smaller residential and commercial properties. Some exclusive agreements are with one agent or company but do not preclude your selling the property yourself. It only excludes your use of other real estate agents. Others grant the agent or company complete and sole rights to the sale. Even if you sell the property yourself, the agent will take a commission. The most effective exclusivity agreement involves your agreeing to give one agent (or company) sole rights to sell the property, but it requires the agent to get the property on the MLS, or Multiple Listing Service, in order to gain a wide exposure to other agents.

With any exclusive agreement, a specific expiration date is important, and indeed a legal requirement in many states. It is also important to include requirements of due diligence on the part of the agent. They do have to work to sell the property. Make sure you go over the entire agreement with the agent so you both understand what is expected of each of you (especially when it comes to advertising the property). Leave no room for misunderstandings.

You can expect your agent to:

* protect your interests
* advertise the property
* open the property for viewings by agents and potential buyers
* keep an eye on your property when you are away
* give advice for property improvement and upkeep
* coordinate with you on repairs and inspections
* check whether or not a buyer is qualified for loans
* oversee the process to ensure that unreasonable demands are not being made
* work with you through the closing

Your agent should also be aware of the following:

* the going price of other properties in the area
* what area buyers are looking for
* financing options
* how to set up and sell notes

You cannot expect your agent to:

* read minds (no one can guess what counter offer will meet the buyer's approval)
* create value (an agent can't make your property worth more than it actually is just because you want it to be so)
* control the bank (an agent can't make the bank approve a purchase price out of whack with an appraisal)
* prices for repairs (agents don't change the rates of contractors and other professionals)

But many an agent will gladly try to accomplish the above in their efforts to serve you and your interests.

One of the biggest assets available to real estate agents is the multiple listing service. The MLS exposes your property to a higher number of potential buyers than your agent could manage alone. Obviously, the more buyers who see your property, the higher chance you have of receiving your asking price (or higher if there are multiple offers). It allows your agent to work with others, with your agent paying a commission to another agent who might help procure a sale. Your agent gets a smaller percentage of the sales price, but can make that percentage up by getting a better price for the property. This use of the MLS may be enough of an asset to you to dictate the use of an agent and it costs you nothing. Your agent gives part of his or her commission to the other agent rather than asking for more from you. In general, MLS is used quite extensively by residential real estate agents, but less so by commercial real estate brokers. Each market is different. But for commercial listings you may need a broker who is in the know, since less of such listings may be widely publicized.

When choosing an agent, find one with whom you are comfortable and whom you trust. Then check out what success the agent has had with previous advertising campaigns (check out sample ads) and what relationship with agent and other agents within and outside the company. In addition, know what functions agents in your area perform. Do they write up offers and work through the closing with title (or escrow) companies, lenders and buyers (or their agents)? Sometimes this is handled by attorneys in certain parts of the country. Be sure to know what services you are getting from your agent.

Chapter 11
Legal Considerations

The legal system has been much maligned in recent years due to frivolous lawsuits, overly litigious attitudes and ridiculous settlements. But seldom does the law work better and make more sense than when it comes to real estate investment and management practices. Real estate investing deals with large sums of money and effectively irreplaceable assets. No one should enter into such deals lightly.

Management of rental properties often deals with the cornerstones of people's lives (and livelihoods) - their homes and businesses. The impacts of misdealings are far-reaching and can be catastrophic for all-involved. The disputes can be emotional. In such dealings, it is best to have well-maintained boundaries, regulations and expectations. Though it may not always feel that way, the legal system provides protection for all involved.

The Contract

The legality of a real estate contract hinges on several factors, all of which involve common sense:

1. A contract must be in writing. No court wants to see a battle of the he-saids/she-saids.
2. Consideration (benefit, interest or value) must be part of the contract. If the land is just given to you with no money or action in return, there is no contract.
3. A contract must be between competent parties. You can't strike a deal to buy crazy Uncle Harold's hundred-acre

ranch for a dollar, even if it is in writing.

4. The contract must represent lawful intent. If you intended a scam, you're busted, even if all the paperwork is pretty as can be.

But these legal requirements don't cover all the common sense inclusions of a contract. For a contract to be valid, it must also include:

1. Agreement. One party cannot unilaterally execute a valid contract. There must be a mutual agreement. Get signatures from all parties involved.

2. Identification of the parties and the property. If a contract doesn't say who is buying what property from whom, it cannot possibly be enforced because the legal system cannot possibly know who to go after for what. Ideally, the contract should list full names and middle initials of the parties (there are a lot of Jim Smiths out there) or the entity name and designation as such (For example: The Seller's Lot, a Wyoming limited liability company). The property designation should be as specific as possible. A legal description is always better than "my cabin in the mountains."

3. Purchase price or a figure that can be arrived at with minimal work, such as "appraised value."

The Sales Package

When you are trying to sell a deal (whether a proposed development or an existing property), be truthful. It's the law. Any pitfalls of the project should be listed. Whatever assumptions you used must be listed in the disclaimer section. It is fine to have pitfalls and assumptions in your sales package, just be honest about them. A savvy buyer will see them anyway and he or she will be unimpressed if you didn't.

In Case of Breach

The practicality of real estate breaches of contract dictates only a few realistic courses of action. If you are the seller and it is the buyer who breaches the contract, you can realistically hope to sue for:

* **Return of earnest money:** keep the buyer's earnest money. You will have at least attempted to construct the contract such that it allows you to keep the earnest money even if you sell the property to another party. If not, you may still prove that it's unfair for the buyer to keep the money since he or she did not keep his or her promise.

* **Specific performance:** the court can force the buyer to follow through with the contract. However, if the buyer can't afford it, well you can't get blood from a brick.

* **Damages:** you have to prove damages to get them, but it's always possible. If you're selling a ski cabin and the buyer backs out just as the snow melts, you're stuck with it until the next snow. That's a real expense, a real damage.

If you are the buyer and the seller is the one to breach the contract, you can realistically hope to sue for:

* **Return of earnest money:** hopefully you set up the contract to keep the earnest money in an escrow account rather than with the seller. If the amount is small, you may be able to get by with small claims court to get your earnest money back.

* **Specific performance:** the court can force the buyer to sell to you.

* **Damages:** though hard to prove, you can hope to have a judge award you the amount of profit you realistically could have seen had the purchase been completed as agreed upon.

Of course, the costs of suing can be upwards of $30,000 and can take up a big chunk of your time. And the outcome is never guaranteed. So take the time upfront, use your lawyer and other consultants to help you before anything is signed. Plan for every contingency your creative mind can imagine. Plan twice and sign once. Vague language, half-listening during negotiations, skimming documents - these are common human foibles. Don't let them cost you the farm (or the office building or the multiplex)!

Part II: Management
Chapter 12
Landlords

Real estate investment and management is one of the very few money-making options for the average person. You don't need a college education. You don't need to be the best at any skill. You don't need years of apprenticeship. You don't need an extreme amount of talent. You don't have to invest a ton of money. You don't need a pedigree. You don't need a ton of employees. You don't need a patent or a copyright or a license or certification. You don't need to spend time away from family and friends. What you do need is an independent spirit and a boatload of common sense. Your real-world experience of reading people, knowing how to look up information, creative problem-solving and organization are all you need to take you from fantasy to the reality of financial independence.

Being a landlord can be emotionally as well as financially fulfilling. Putting a roof over a person's head is rewarding. Watching a family turn your house into their home can be awe-inspiring. Creating a haven from the harsh realities of everyday life of your tenants is no small feat. However, being a landlord does not come without its baggage, costs and stigmas.

Fact vs. Fiction

Landlord. Not a word that connotes visions of empathy or ethics. Most of us see the word "landlord" and we think "slumlord." Our minds flash back to news reports and movie depictions of rat-infested buildings crumbling around the hapless, but good-hearted occupants inside. We imagine the greedy building owner alone in his mansion, huddled over his mountain of cash, cackling like the villain he is, planning new and better ways to make the lives of his tenants more miserable.

Necessary Skills

Your job as landlord entails a whole lot more than just collecting the rent every month and fixing the occasional sink. You must be a savvy businessperson, researching and choosing the right property, negotiating contracts, creating profitable rental contracts, cutting expenses, understanding and keeping up with tax and legal issues, organizing office policies and setting up accurate accounting practices. You must also be a handyman or excellent manager and negotiator of contract help. But most of all, you must be adept at dealing with people.

When it comes down to rental property management, it is the tenants who will make or break the operation. You need to be able to choose the best tenants, mediate disputes, set down the rules and stick to them, find ways to keep good tenants, handle evictions and negotiate rental contract terms.

Responsibilities

If your tenant breaks the rules, he or she can be evicted. But if you break the rules, you can be sued. Every state has minimum requirements regarding habitability of a building. Some are stricter than others, but all carry obligations with them. Talk to your lawyer or otherwise find out the laws for your state and then do what is required and more. Keep good tenants happy. Avoid lawsuits. While the lawyers do, landlords almost never make money in legal disputes.

Beyond suing, in many states your tenants can deduct repairs from their rent, leave without notice and stop paying rent if you aren't keeping the building up to your state's legal standards. None of these scenarios does you any good. Not only does it affect short-term and long-term cash flow, your time and energy are eaten up.

The time when the landlord only owed the tenant the legal minimum and only performed repairs and improvements spelled out in the rental contract left the way of disco and platform shoes. Since the 1970s the implied warranty of habitability, in most states, has maintained that the landlord must keep the property up to the fitness present when the tenant moved in. You must keep up with repairs and maintenance.

The definition of habitability differs state by state, and even city by city. Some areas use only those regulations set out in existing housing laws (building codes, health codes and the like). This form of regulation is nice in that you, as landlord, know exactly what your obligations are.

Other areas use the standard of "fit for human occupancy." Obviously this can be a subjective interpretation. Expectations of the court may exceed the local housing codes. Some common examples of fit and habitable conditions are running water (hot and cold), working electrical and heating equipment, clean and well-maintained common areas, working toilets and sinks, garbage and debris removal. Depending on where the building is located, such services as snow removal or extermination may be required as well.

Even in states that have chosen not to dictate an implied warranty of habitability, a landlord must take care of the building to be sure it is up to code. And even if there are no codes in your area, you're still not off the hook. The common-law concept of "covenant of quiet enjoyment" is enforceable in every state. A landlord must maintain his or her building in a way that does not interfere or destroy the tenant's ability to use and enjoy his or her rented area. Therefore, you have to take care of bug infestations, keep the plumbing and heating working, supply working electrical outlets and repair broken or rotting staircases, floors, walls, ceilings and roofs. Consider keeping the property maintained according to how you would expect to be treated as a tenant.

Go to your local housing authority and find out what building and housing codes exist in your area. Check to make sure you understand which authorities override one another. State and local codes may differ. If they do in your case, you need to know which code rules. The stricter code usually prevails, but not always.

There are always exemptions to laws. Single-family, owner-occupied structures are often not required to meet local or state housing codes. Other buildings may be grandfathered in - not required to meet the standards if built before a specified date.

However, you shouldn't expect the tenant to put up with a barely habitable or unattractive building just because of your legal rights. The tenant is the customer, and if you don't take care of him or her, someone else will. Rental property can be pretty competitive and vacancies can eat away at your profitability like a cancer. Be proactive about your tenants' happiness whenever and wherever you can. Ongoing property improvements mean ongoing rental contract improvements and it is the rental contract improvements that make you money.

Restrictions

There is a whole host of restrictions put on landlords to protect tenants. These will be covered in greater detail later in this book. Ignore such restrictions at your own peril. Fines and even prison may await you if you do.

Never discriminate when choosing or interacting with tenants. If you're unsure what constitutes discrimination (or even if you think you know), check with your lawyer to find out all local and federal regulations that apply.

Be careful with evictions. You cannot physically remove a tenant or his or her belongings without following the pertinent legal requirements first. You cannot change the locks or shut off the utilities to force a tenant out, nor do you have the right to force a tenant to clean the premises or obey any laws.

You can't go into a rented unit without appropriate notice (except in cases of imminent danger, such as with a fire, gas leak or busted pipe), with the term of prior notice being different state to state (but usually 24 to 48 hours). Give the notice in writing whenever you can and always have a reason. Nor can you remove a tenant's personal property (including pets and cars, etc.) without permission. This is stealing. To protect yourself from wrongful claims of stealing (and other complaints), it is best to bring someone else with you as a witness whenever you have to enter a unit (especially if the tenant has been uncooperative). Also, without notice to the tenants, never let someone else into the apartment when the tenant is absence. Even building inspectors need permission or a warrant. The only exception would be in an emergency or in the case of police officers in pursuit of a criminal.

If you need to show an occupied unit for purposes of renting or selling, try to work out arrangements with the current occupant. There are laws governing this category of entry. Know them. A tenant's right to privacy cannot be violated just because he or she is not renewing a rental contract or because you are ready to move on. Give the current tenant as much prior notice of your plans as you can. Common courtesy goes a long way here (as does common sense). You really have nothing to lose by being accommodating and you could avoid a lawsuit.

You can't do whatever you want with your property. You can't destroy it or let it sit empty for long periods. Nor can you use it for purposes other than those set out by local zoning boards and the like. You can't change a property protected by a state or local historical society without permission. There are even restrictions on which repairs you can make yourself. Many require that the person performing the repairs is licensed for those repairs.

Once again, be sure you know the law. Know your legal responsibilities and restrictions imposed upon you. It can get complicated and ignorance is never an excuse.

Rights

There will be days when you feel as if you have no rights and that you are at the mercy of your tenants. This isn't true. Keep in contact with your tenants, have an ironclad rental contract, maintain the property and you won't feel so much like the victim of your own investment.

As a property owner you have the right to rent the property, of course. Zoning ordinances and city or county laws may dictate the use of the rental property, but you do have the right to rent. Check with state and local governments to be sure you can use the building for the uses you have in mind. Do this before you even consider buying the property.

You have money rights. You can break even, operate at a loss, make a profit, keep your property for yourself, rent it out, sell it - the choices are yours. You may require tenants to pay their own utilities (as long as there are separate meters). You may charge a security deposit and then keep it if the tenant damages your property.

You have rights regarding who you choose as tenants. Have a rental application, check the information given. You can refuse tenancy to people who lie on that application. You can designate the property as an animal-free zone (except service animals such as seeing eye dogs). You may make criminal, credit and former eviction histories part of the rental application for screening purposes (however, watch out for discrimination).

You have the right to legally defend yourself. If claims are brought against you (such as housing code violations), you have the right to a court hearing to dispute such claims.

You have maintenance rights. Most repairs can be performed by you or your repair personnel. In some cases, only certain repairs may be performed by licensed professionals (such as wiring by electricians). Absent such requirements, you and your team can do what is needed.

Types of Managers

There are three primary categories of managers:

* Owner occupant
* Absentee owner
* Hired Property Manager

Owner Manager

The owner occupant manager is the owner who lives at the premises while managing it. He or she is a constant force in the life of the tenants. Some tenants like this because they find their concerns are addressed more quickly. Others dislike it because they feel as if Big Brother is watching them.

In general, when the owner lives on the premises, the neighborhood benefits. Maintenance and cleanup become routine, disturbances are dealt with more quickly (the owner is disturbed along with the neighbors and does not have to be called) and the property feels more a part of the wider community.

However, being an owner occupant manager can mean being on-call 24 hours a day, seven days a week. Because you are right there, tenants and neighbors feel you should deal with any concerns or complaints right now. If you were an absentee owner manager, tenants and neighbors would be more likely to wait until customary business hours to call on you. It is always best, in either scenario, to have in your rental contracts an outline as to when and where to contact you. Set up business hours then explain to tenants (and neighbors if necessary) that you have a life outside work just like them. Make it clear that just as they would not call their car mechanic or banker after hours, they should not call you (except in cases of emergency).

Another problem that can occur when you live on the premises you manage is a tendency to form personal relationships with tenants. This is fine when everything is running smoothly. But it can be a big problem when you are trying to collect late rent or, even worse, find yourself having to evict a tenant who has become a friend. It is much easier to keep the business a business when you are not running into those you manage in the laundry room, in the halls or in the parking lot. In short, it is much easier to separate your business life from your personal life when you are not living at the premises you manage.

If you inherit tenants, take the time to go meet each of them face to face. Sending a letter can be great for notification of your terms, your experience and your expectations and you should send one. But it is that face to face interaction that will put the tenants at ease and set the tone for your relationships.

Hired Manager

You might choose to leave the whole shebang up to a property manager who takes care of day-to-day operations for you. Maybe you live too far from your property or your day job takes up all your time or you simple don't feel confident that you know how to do the job of managing a rental property. Whatever your reasons, there are lots of people out there willing to help you - for a fee.

The contract is the document in which the fees, services, rights and duties will be laid out. It is important to include the term of service (with start and end dates), the pay rate (hourly, full-time, part-time, salary, reduced rent) what is expected of each side (take care to detail the manager's duties), how and when the manager can spend your money (including what happens when there isn't enough money to cover the bills), what paperwork will be prepared for you and what paperwork and money you will provide to the manager.

You can hire an individual as property manager or a management company. Either will take care of finding (and evicting) tenants, make sure necessary repairs are made, handle the money coming in and going out, deal with tenant complaints and keep up the accounting. A good manager should strive to keep vacancies down, decrease incidents of late payments, ensure improvements are on schedule and on-going, keep complaints to a minimum and increase your profits.

The person you hire, either as an individual or through a management company, should be licensed, if such requirements exist in your state, and that license needs to be good in the state in which the property is located. Generally, you don't need to be licensed to manage your own property.

Some real estate professional groups offer management designations for their members who choose to further their professional qualifications. The National Association of Realtors offers a Certified Property Manager designation for its members. Institute of

Real Estate Management members may become Accredited Resident Managers and firms may be listed as Accredited Management Organizations. The Building Owners and Managers Association offers the title of Real Property Administrator.

Following are just a few things to look for in a property manager:

* Good reputation - ask around and check references
* License
* Familiarity with local laws and regulations regarding real estate
* Sufficient staff - a single person may be fine for a small property, but larger ones will need more. Be sure whatever your property needs, the manager can accommodate it.
* Experience with properties like yours
* Clean driving, credit and criminal history

When you hire an individual (rather than a management company) he or she is referred to as a resident manager and may either live on the premises or simply have a rental office there.

Whichever type of property manager you decide upon, it is best to let the tenants know in writing about the position. They need to know if he or she is empowered to deliver legal documents on your behalf. It is also a good deal to take the manager around and introduce him personally to the tenants. Keep in mind that good property management entails good people management. The more emotionally or psychologically invested your tenants feel in the property, the better care they will take of your investment. Building loyalty and personal ease with tenants will prevent many common management problems.

A good property manager may also be a good consultant. He or she should have knowledge of market and economic forces and may be able to advise you on appropriate rent rates, rental contract contents and the like. He or she should also have valuable business contacts - bankers, repairmen, inspectors, etc.

Regardless of whether you choose a property manager or

you choose to manage the property yourself, you are still the one liable for problems. Let the manager handle routine operations but do not abdicate your decision-making authority. Rental property is not something you just buy and forget. Don't let "out of sight" mean "out of mind" or you might soon find yourself out of business.

Each style of management - owner occupant, absentee owner or hired property manager - has its pros and cons, but choosing which to use will most likely come down to your personality. So think carefully about your lifestyle, your people skills, finances and time constraints before making a choice.

Protect Yourself

If you choose to hire a manager, cover your assets. You will be an employer. As such, you will want to be sure that both you and your new employee understand all landlord-tenant and eviction laws applicable in your area. Get a copy to your manager and keep one for yourself. You can end up in court over the actions of your manager because he or she represents you. Also check that your insurance covers illegal acts by your employee.

Becoming an employer means entering a whole new arena of liability and obligation. You must pay income, Social Security and Medicare taxes, provide at least a minimum wage and follow regulations regarding overtime. This goes whether the manager is being compensated through a salary, hourly wage or reduced rent. Don't try to label your manager an independent contractor to avoid your obligations. The only time the manager might be considered an independent is if he or she manages several different properties.

Before you hire anyone, contact the IRS and the United States Labor Department (Wage and Hour Division) and the state labor department to familiarize yourself with all applicable laws, regulations and guidelines. Or use a CPA or payroll service to set up all the accounts.

The Rental Office

    As a landlord you may find it necessary to exercise (or even learn) an entirely new set of skills. Unless you hire out some jobs, you will be the bookkeeper, accountant, office manager, receptionist, mail clerk, errand boy, banker, salesperson, advertising expert, repairman, janitor and mediator. Organization is the heart of efficiency. Efficiency is the heart of a small business.

    Your investment is a business. Treat it as such. Take it seriously so others might take you seriously. Set up a business office if at all feasible. A computer can be an excellent tool for real estate owners. There are a number of good property management programs to assist in streamlining and tracking your business operations. Consider a phone line designated strictly for business, especially if working from home. Try out phones and see if a speaker or hands-free headset work for you. Voicemail or an answering machine are a must. You never want to miss a call. Most tenants want a place now. They won't be calling back. A fax machine will speed up all your paper interactions (getting credit reports and other applicant information). A cell phone rounds out the great communication triumvirate: phone, fax and cell. And a small desktop copier will save you the time and hassle of constantly having to run to the local copy shop. A mail drop box will ensure tenants can drop off rent after business hours (which is when it is more convenient for them, less so for you).

    To keep you organized, invest in file cabinets (preferably locking ones) and enough file folders to handle the constant mound of paperwork you will be struggling to control. Similarly, consider a paper shredder to get rid of obsolete but sensitive materials (you may also hire a shredding service). A printing calculator or 10-key will help you when dealing with long columns of numbers. You never want to be in the position of having to re-enter 100 numbers because one of them was mis-entered. Bulletin boards (cord or dry-erase) help you maintain control of your business. Having tasks out where you can see them decreases the chance of forgetting about them. Dedicate one board just for duplicate keys to all your units so you don't have to scramble or go to a locksmith each time someone loses their keys. Consider a locked cabinet for the keys to insure their protection.

If it saves you time use the technology resources that are available. Word processing, a spreadsheet program and a good accounting program are the basics. You may choose to also invest in graphics capabilities for advertising purposes, but you may also choose to hire that out. Be sure you purchase a computer that offers enough memory and speed to allow your business to grow. E-mail and Internet access are helpful, as is an electronic organizer you can synchronize with your desktop PC. Don't wait until you need a computer to learn to use one. You never want to find yourself in the position of trying to learn a new skill in the middle of a crisis.

Other skills you will need to learn include time management, prioritization, diplomacy, money management and confidence. These aren't really things you can hire someone else to do for you; they must exist within you. If they don't, take yourself to a bookstore and start scanning the self-help and business sections for books that appeal to you. Go On-line and search the Web. Talk to other landlords. Acquire these skills or let your business die trying.

The Home Office

If you do choose to work your rental business from home, work hard to separate your work life from your home life. Keep regular business hours, install a dedicated phone line for the business and if at all possible, have at least an entire room dedicated to use as an office. If done properly, you can deduct the percentage expenses (mortgage, utilities, etc.) associated with your office as a business expense. Work with your accountant to take advantage of this write off. Make sure the room has a door and hang a "do not disturb" sign on it whenever you are working to ensure everyone else in your home knows to take your work as seriously as you do.

Of course you won't want to be meeting tenants at your home. This leads to several challenges. It will be harder to collect rents when tenants can't drop it off with you. You will spend a lot of time arranging meetings and then traveling to and from them. You will lose time when the people with whom you are schedule to meet don't show up. You will be dragging paperwork to and from these meetings, always in danger of forgetting something and losing even more time in retrieval.

You will, however, save money and have the luxury of flexibility. No extra rent, fewer supplies, tax deductions. And when you're at home you can work when you want - during the baby's nap, between your favorite TV shows, on the treadmill. You can work in your pajamas, take a break for a walk or a nap and play Solitaire on the computer without fear of reprisal.

Your tenants need not know you are working from home, however. A dedicated phone line, professional sounding voicemail and a P.O. box go a long way toward the illusion of an outside office. You can even make up an imposing company name to have printed on all your forms and correspondence. It depends on your style.

In short, what you lose in efficiency do you gain in flexibility? Does your personality allow for that tradeoff? Are you a Type-A personality that will be driven nuts by the constant interruptions of working at home? Are you disciplined enough to keep from creating your own interruptions?

Chapter 13
Tenants

You can't get rent without renters. When you have renters, you have people - and all the ups and downs that dealing with members of our species entails. No two people think alike and no two people view the world through the same lens. We all bring our own baggage to our interactions with one another. It is easy to get sucked into pettiness and emotional responses when dealing with the landlord/tenant relationship. But this is a business. Use your empathy and your business sense to keep your operation running smoothly.

Responsibilities

From the last chapter, you are probably lamenting that it seems all the responsibilities of the landlord-tenant relationship are yours. While the heavier burden is definitely on the landlord side there are good reasons. As the landlord you are in a position of power. And it is the person in power who carries the weight of fairness. After all, what really can your tenants do? They can irritate you, cost you money in repairs and possibly court costs, hassle you, but they can't put you out in the street. You, on the other hand, have power over one of the basic human necessities - shelter. You have the power to leave a person, or even a whole family, homeless. And that awesome level of power can be abused. The bulk of landlord-tenant laws are not meant to make your job more difficult but simply to protect tenants from unscrupulous property owners.

Still, tenants do have responsibilities. These responsibilities may change city to city, state to state, but they do exist. A tenant may have to maintain the property's habitability, safety and cleanliness. The tenant is responsible for damage. If he or she breaks it, he or she has to fix it (or pay to have it fixed). He or she cannot unreasonably burden the utilities (overloading electrical outlets, attempting to use the toilet as a garbage receptacle).

If you think your responsibility is an unfair burden, there is a simple solution: make the tenant responsible for more through the rental contract. Again, the power is yours. If you want the tenant to be responsible for keeping the flower garden alive, fine, put it in the rental contract. If you want the tenant to notify you when he or she is out of town in the winter (to avoid bursting pipes), fine, put it in the rental contract. Whatever is in the rental contract (short of violating existing laws, such as those regarding discrimination and the right to privacy) goes. You make the rental contract; you make the rules. Don't whine about your responsibilities.

Revel in your power. Use your power to make the situation equitable and rewarding for your tenants as well as yourself. The level of personal fulfillment you will find will far outweigh the work involved.

Rights

The tenant has a lot of rights. Sometimes it may seem as if he or she has all the rights. But don't despair, most of a tenant's rights come down to common sense, if not common courtesy. Think about it, if you say you have a room for rent and someone comes by looking like they can't afford it, do they still have the right to see the room and/or submit a rental application? Of course they do. You can't discriminate. Nor should you want to. You are in business to make money and improve your life, not to validate your own (or anyone else's) prejudice.

Do you have the right to keep security deposits even if the tenant leaves the unit clean and in good repair. No. Can anyone use video and digital cameras with date notations to show before and after conditions to justify keeping security deposits? Yes.

Do you have the right to share a tenant's information on their application with friends, neighbors or telemarketers? Of course not. Would you want anyone to whom you give such information to share it? Of course not. You also don't have the right to barge into the unit unannounced, even if you do own it. Tenants have rights to privacy just like you. You must give notice for entry, eviction and inspections.

Tenants have the right to safe, clean properties (were you planning on being a slumlord?) and can reasonably modify the space for quiet use and enjoyment. In many states they can withhold rent if you don't make necessary repairs.

Most landlord-tenant relationships do well by following the Golden Rule - treat others as you would have them treat you. You don't want them treating the property like a dump, so make basic upkeep a priority. You don't want them contacting you at home, so don't contact them at work. You want to be able to get in for maintenance, so don't barge in unannounced. You will set the tone. Everything you do and say will be a message as to how you view your business. If you take it seriously and have pride in the property you will increase the chances that your tenants will do the same. Treat it as a slumlord would and you will find yourself owning a slum.

Chapter 14

Finding the Right Tenant

Your building is a sight to behold. It is a strong, well-maintained rental magnet. It was a bargain and promises great profit. All you've got to do now is throw the keys up in the air and start filing rental agreements, right? Of course not. You would no sooner rent your property to a stranger than you would invite a stranger to come live with you. In order to actually ever see profitable rental property, you must have three components working in harmony:

1. Desirable property
2. Efficient, knowledgeable management
3. Good tenants

And what makes a good tenant? Someone who loves your property as if it were their own, who has the means and the desire to pay rent on time and who doesn't mind taking care of a few problems his or herself.

You don't need tenants who see your property as just a convenient stopover. Transience can kill a marginal investment as the costs of vacancies soon outweigh the income of the rented units.

You don't need someone who doesn't care what their home or office looks like, such as someone who let the carpet go to pot, let the plants die, watch as water ruins the drywall and cracks the foundation without a word to you. You will not have continual access to your units and will need to rely on tenants to alert you to small problems that could become catastrophes. While you don't want someone calling you every hour, you don't want someone who will let the big things slide either.

Similarly, it is in your best interest to find tenants who can (and will) take care of the average nuisances themselves. Find tenants who will try a plunger before a plumber, replace a fuse before calling an electrician. Handy tenants can be worth their weight in reduced rent.

Setting the Rent

The amount of rent your charge is not a function of your wants or needs, but rather a complicated dance of supply and demand, cost and profit. In order to break even you will have to know your costs inside and out. This means more than the mortgage. Operating costs, taxes, permit costs, insurance rates, renovation and upkeep costs, accountant fees and all the costs that brought you to the sale to begin with (broker, attorney and contractor costs) will all need to be accounted for in your figuring. And until you get into it you'll nickel and dime costs there are in running a rental property.

Your rent should cover all your expenses associated with managing the building and offer a percentage return on the costs you incurred in purchasing the building. But don't forget inflation - that bug-eyed hobgoblin of commerce. You will need to routinely raise rents to keep inflation from eating away at your profits until there are none.

Not only do you need to know how much you need in order to break even on your investment, you also need to know what the market can bear. Identify security deposit and rental rates for your area. Keep your eyes on the rental section of the newspapers (as well as any specialty papers that cater to your building type) to see what the going rental rate is. The local housing authority also tracks such information. And you may want to ask other landlords how much their tenants pay, but many will want to keep that information private. There is nothing wrong with inquiring as if you were a potential tenant rather than a potential competitor.

When comparing your property to others, take into account

as many amenities as you can think of.

For residential property, consider information such as:

> * neighborhood desirability
> * distance to shopping, schools and entertainment
> * age of the neighborhood
> * views
> * age of the property
> * square footage
> * number of bedrooms
> * number of bathrooms
> * size of yard
> * availability of parking
> * condition of common areas
> * appliances included
> * laundry facilities
> * exercise facilities
> * pool/spa
> * security

For commercial property, consider:

> * size of the unit
> * desirability of the location
> * proximity to transportation corridors
> * age of the building
> * parking
> * security
> * condition of entrances
> * condition of public spaces
> * views
> * distance to support industries
> * janitorial services

Know the region. In some areas a pool is a necessity for an apartment complex. Or maybe snow removal is necessary for an office complex. Know what your tenants will expect for the rent they will be asked to pay. By comparing your amenities to others' at the same time you compare rents, you should gain a good understanding of these expectations. Salesmanship can be boiled down to nothing more than giving people what they want. Solve their problems and they will buy your product. By studying the market (amenities, deposits and rents), you discover your clients' wants and challenges. You are then armed to make their lives better.

The local, regional and national economy will also become much more interesting to you now that you own rental property. You will be constantly evaluating economic trends to see what affect they might have on your property and profitability. You may not become an economist, but in time you will come to look like one.

Advertising

When you were going through the research process necessary to figure out how much to charge for rent you should have drawn some safe conclusions as to what your target renters want. Remember, you want to solve their problems. Do your target residential renters want family homes that allow kids and pets? Fine, you can do that (using a rental contract with the right reward/punishment system). Do they want garages? You took that into consideration when you were buying because you know that the best way to attract quality renters is to purchase the kinds of building they want to rent. If you want families, buy family homes (three-bedroom, two-bath, yard, garage). If you want large numbers in small areas, try apartments near universities (but prepared for high turnover and serious cleaning deposits).

If your commercial market is sadly lacking in adequate parking, buy a building with enough land (or garage potential) to compensate. If your ideal commercial renters are image-conscious, put a little money into making the building look modern and inviting. If you want high-tech renters, be sure your communication technology is up to date. Everyone wants the higher ceilings and reliable utilities that come with newer buildings. This may be important to note if your building has been upgraded to make it superior to other buildings of similar age in your area.

What makes your property unique? Does your single-family home have a pool or a fireplace? Vaulted ceilings? Does your turn-of-the-century brick bungalow come with modern plumbing and electrical? Is there a spectacular view? Sunken tubs?

What sets your commercial property apart? How many windows are there? Are there kitchen facilities? Covered parking? Is it build-to-suit?

Then once you start your advertising campaign be sure to highlight all these amenities that make your property superior to those of your competitors. List the property's best features first to capture your target renter's attention. Remember what caught your attention when you were scouting for investment property. Those same features will likely (though not always) attract renters as well.

Don't be shy with the superlatives, but don't lie. No one will rent property sight unseen and any lies (or ridiculous exaggerations) will be found out. You can be prosecuted for them. Likewise, never discriminate in any way in your advertising. Don't say you're looking for single men or whites only or anything else that violates the Fair Housing Act. Don't give offense. It's that simple. Don't say your rental is on "the good side of town" or in a "low-crime area." Be very careful and use a common sense filter when you word your advertising.

In today's media-saturated world, there are many media to choose from for your campaign. Radio, television, newspapers, flyers, for-rent signs, Internet, E-mail - all are viable options. Choose the advertising media that will reach the best renters in your target market for the least cost, always taking into account your needs. You likely don't need to attract 200 renters to apply for your single-family home or small office complex.

For this reason, television may not be right for you. It reaches a lot of people, but is expensive. If you do have multiple units to rent and choose television, remember that VHF and non-network-affiliated stations are cheaper than network-affiliated

Radio is less expensive but much more narrowly targeted. This can be good and bad. If you know precisely which stations your target demographic prefers (and you may if you hire the right agency to handle your campaign), then you can get a lot of bang for your buck. But if you are planning on a mass appeal, shotgun sort of approach, you may be looking at to high a cost for your small number of properties.

Flyers are a cheap alternative to television and radio. Bulletin boards in Laundromats, grocery stores, gyms, power poles and any other public place that allows posting is a potential source of renters. Get to know the staff at housing offices for local colleges and the larger businesses that have such offices. Let them know when you have a unit for rent and be sure to notify them when the unit is off the market. You may also want to hire students to pass out flyers around different neighborhoods whose demographics fit your target. Always find out if you need permission before you post and then get it. Flyers are a sort of hit-and-miss proposition, but the hits may be worth it. Of course, don't forget to take the flyers down when the unit is rented.

To get the word out only to those who are actively looking for rentals, try the newspaper classifieds. But be brief; you will be paying by the word. Likewise with rental guides. They charge fee, but target active rental seekers. While you pay a fee for the listing, the guides are distributed to local establishments at no cost.

The Internet is yet another advertising option open to you. Some existing sites will advertise your rental for a fee, some only require you be a member of the site. And you can always design your own specialized site. You might hire someone to design a site for you or get software to walk you through the process. A very inexpensive but high quality web design firm that assists landlords is found at www.iqandesign.com.

If you live in a landlord's market, you may have to do no more than place a "For Rent" sign on the front lawn or window and wait for your phone to ring. Some locales are in such demand that people know to drive around those areas when they are looking to find rentals (residential or commercial). In some areas, such as San Francisco's desirable Pacific Heights district, apartments are rented within hours of the "For Rent" sign going up.

You might also try word-of-mouth. Put the word out with friends and associates that you have space for rent. To sweeten the deal, you can offer a finder's fee for anyone who brings renters your way. Fishing for tenants this way tends to net renters similar to the people who are recruiting them. So choose your word-of-mouth originators as you would a renter.

Rental Applications

Never rent without a rental application. Whether your property is residential or commercial, be choosy about your tenants. Take the time to choose, rather than later having to take the time to remove a tenant. Not only will you save time; you'll save money and energy as well. Spend your money making money rather than eliminating hassles your own negligence created.

Your rental application should ask for information on:

* Name, current address, phone number
* Identification (driver's license, social security number - always get two forms)
* The applicant's finances
* Credit history (permission to get such. This requires joining a credit reporting agency for a fee, but it is usually worth it and you may choose to pass the cost onto the applicant. It's your choice. But never give out any information you receive on this report to anyone but the applicant him or herself.)
* Applicant's rental history (where he or she last lived and how long he or she rented the last unit) including evictions.
* Employment history
* Contact information for emergencies
* Number of people and/or pets to be living in the unit
* Criminal history (arrests as well as convictions - you don't want a lot of police visits to your property)
* References (but remember that references are useless if you don't actually check them) Call previous landlords and ask about the applicant if the tenant is still renting use your instinct to judge whether the current landlord wants to unload a problem tenant.

When qualifying a residential renter, check to see that the rent is not more than 30 percent of the renter's income. This federal guideline is a useful one. A tenant who has to choose between rent and food or other necessities is not the kind of stable renter you want. He or she may be the nicest person you know, but don't put them in the position of making such choices. Neither of you will be happy.

Some applicants may balk at a thorough check of their background and finances. That's fine. They might have something to hide; they might not. Others might welcome your thoroughness because it shows you care about your property - their home. It also means that there is a good chance that their new home isn't filled with felons and scofflaws. You might choose to make exceptions to what you think is a perfect applicant. That's fine. But know to whom you are renting. Get the application.

Ideally, you will want to have your first conversation with the prospective tenant over the phone. Ask a few preliminary questions to see if he or she is the type of person who would fit with your project. Ask if the applicant has ever been evicted, how much he or she can afford for rent, what he or she does for a living and for how long, how many people will be living at the premises, etc. You might think that this is the time to show the unit, but hold off. Get the rental application first. There is no use in your showing the unit to someone who can't afford it. It's disappointing for the potential renter and a waste of your time. The application also provides the potential for added security. You have a name, address and phone number. Just in case.

Security can be a sticky subject when showing the unit. You may choose to have the applicant meet you at your office or in a public place (if you have no office) to fill out the application. Check the information then let the applicant view the unit without you - get a deposit, give the applicant the key and set up a time to meet back. This scenario does leave your unit vulnerable, but you should know enough from the application to feel your property is safe in the applicant's hands. If you are uneasy, consider accompanying the applicant to the unit. If this does not feel safe either, considering taking someone with you. Introduce this person as your business partner. Yet another alternative would be to set one time for all prospective tenants to view the property at the same time.

Remember to treat everyone the same throughout the process. Discrimination is not just bad business, it's illegal. And the person you choose to discriminate against may not be a simple applicant. He or she may be a checker hired by an agency to test how you treat different categories of people. If you require a key deposit for one applicant, do so with all. If you buy coffee for one applicant, buy one for all. Be very very careful. Routine is the great protector against discrimination. Have a system for every part of your management process (the application, interview, collecting rent, evictions) and then use it consistently.

Common courtesy is necessary when showing occupied units. Only bring applicants by during reasonable hours, preferably when the current renter isn't there (you may not want the applicant to have the current tenant's input) and always give the applicant enough time to thoroughly inspect the unit without unduly intruding upon the current renter's life.

The Interview

Not all owners/managers go to the lengths of conducting an applicant interview. Some consider a thorough and thoroughly checked rental application enough information upon which to base their approval/denial decisions. These managers often (and should to ensure there has not been any discrimination) accept qualified tenants on a first-come, first-served basis. Others have an interview process that surpasses the most vigorous employment interview. The choice is yours and, as with all others, will be a function of your needs and management style.

If you do choose to perform an interview, again be aware of fair housing laws. Don't discriminate. Interview everyone in the same manner. Protect yourself with consistency.

The interview provides an opportunity to go over your rental agreement in excruciating detail. You want all prospective tenants to know how seriously you take your contract and that it is legally binding. Before a renter signs, he or she needs to understand each detail in the contract. You need to be sure he or she understands it. Be prepared to answer any questions that might arise from your discussion. Be sure you have allotted enough time for the interview to allow for adequate explanations.

If more than one person will be living in the unit, it would be best to meet all involved. If it is going to be a husband and wife meet both of them. Even kids. You can learn a lot about the applicants by watching how they interact with one another.

During the interview you will be trying to get to know the applicant. This requires listening and observing. Pay attention to what is said and what isn't. You know by now what sort of tenant you want to see in your property. If you're looking for stable families, beware of parents who don't ask about schools or parks. Watch out for long, involved explanations about finances, evictions and job losses. Ironically, too much detail can be a sign of a less-than-truthful applicant.

Ask prospective tenants about their jobs (where they work, why, whether or not they like their job and are planning on staying where they are). Ask why they want to live in the part of town where you own property. Ask about their family, hobbies and interests.

While you are interviewing the potential renter, keep in mind that he or she is interviewing you. What do you want them to take away from the interaction? Your best bet is to make your rules and regulations clear. You want all candidates to take you seriously and to respect your authority. Property management is not the place to make buddies.

Choosing Among Tenants

The applications are complete, the interviews are finished and you have your perfected rental agreement all ready for your new tenant's signature. Finally. Now you need to notify your chosen tenant. But you also need to notify those tenants whose applications you are rejecting.

If you use a first-come, first-serve selection process, the approval/rejection process will be much easier than if you went through the comparative interview process. You will have (of course) told prospective tenants about your selection process before this time. Still, some of the applicants will want to know why their applications were rejected. Your answers had better be devoid of any hint of discrimination. Negative credit reports and flat-out lies on the application are sure-fire (and safe) rejection material.

To keep to your consistency goals, prepare a multiple choice rejection form you can send to applicants. This allows you to go over your reasons with your lawyer and then just check the appropriate box before sending the form out. Applicants will know why their applications were rejected and you will have given the notice objectively and professionally.

For credit problems, your credit agency should have a form for you to use. You must supply the applicant with the information so that he or she can check and possibly challenge what the report says. Because of all the privacy issues involved with credit reports, it is best for you to talk with the credit agency and/or your lawyer to be sure you understand your rights and obligations.

Chapter 15
Dealing with Tenants

You paid for a building, but what you bought was tenants. And all the other joys and hassles that can come with them. If it's been a while since you've been in a position of authority, you might want to brush up. If you've never really managed people before, you might want to learn some skills. Or hire a manager.

There are plenty of sources to teach you about effective management. Book stores, the Internet, college courses, small business development authorities and the like. It shouldn't cost a lot of money to get your skills up to par. Invest the time. Invest it in your business. Invest it in your tenants.

The Rental Contract

Both the lease and the rental agreement are rental contracts. Both are contracts binding you and the tenant in agreement as to duties and responsibilities concerning rental of your space. They can be simple or complex, but should be in writing. A lease for over one year in length must be in writing to be enforceable. The agreement should be thoroughly understood by both parties. Many a landlord-tenant problem can be prevented by understanding what it is you are both agreeing to.

The primary difference between a rental agreement and a lease is the time commitment listed within. A rental agreement is short-term (usually month-to-month), whereas a lease is long-term (usually a year) with fixed start and end dates.

A well-prepared rental contract can help tenants feels stable.

They understand their boundaries. By signing the contract, they have committed to their end of the bargain.

Ideally you took the time and thoroughly researched your tenants during the application and/or interview stage and have now selected the right chosen few to add to the synergy and profitability of your property. Now begins the indoctrination process. The rental contract is only part of that indoctrination.

You need to be sure the tenant knows how to take care of the property. Maintenance knowledge is not the tenant's responsibility. But having tenants who can and will maintain your property will save you money, time and increase your tenant's feeling of ownership in the property. With that feeling comes pride in the premises - the kind of pride that leads to a tenant taking care of your property without you ever saying a word.

Some landlords have full maintenance manuals for their tenants, covering every subject from changing a light bulb to unplugging a toilet. Other landlords pay for a series of short classes. For some landlords, it is the primary criteria by which they choose tenants. Some landlords offer decreased rents to tenants who take care of maintenance. Some offer nothing, but make maintenance a requirement nonetheless. Whatever you expect, put it in the rental contract.

Tenants aren't mind readers. Neither are landlords. Put all your expectations in the contract so there can be no misunderstanding down the line.

The rental contract should spell out all rewards offered to tenants for good behavior. Do you offer a discount if the rent is paid on time? Do you allow modifications of the premises to long-term tenants? If a tenant is willing to take on routine maintenance his or herself, do you offer a discounted deposit program (some tenants will do the cleanup of a vacant property before they move in if you waive the cleaning deposit) or pay for supplies? Whatever your reward program, be consistent.

The contract should also spell out all the punishments that you are willing to dole out for unacceptable tenant behavior. This can range from extra costs for late rent to eviction for bringing in a roommate without consent. Consistency is even more important with your punishment program than with your reward program. Making one exception could jeopardize your authority and undermine the entire program.

Don't worry about being too harsh with your rules and offending a good tenant. Good tenants are listening for the rewards in your program. They aren't really worried about your penalties because they fully intend to be good tenants. But don't make your program so restrictive that even a good tenant will have a hard time meeting your rules. Life happens. There needs to be some measure of flexibility in every program to accommodate the bad things that sometimes happen to good tenants. You're dealing with people, not drones.

Try to accommodate some of your tenant's wants if they do not interfere with your overall program. It is not convenient for every tenant to pay rent on the first of the month. It shouldn't be any skin off your nose to let tenants help choose their rental due date. Of course, once that date is set, there is even less excuse for being late. Giving in on the simple things allows the renter to feel like part of the team. If you want to rent to adults, treat renters with dignity and respect. Most people will try to live up to your high expectations. Why not help give them the opportunity to do just that?

Some subjects to include in the rental contract include:

* **The basics:** your name, the tenant's name (including trade name), address of property, etc.

* **Rent:** how much (the high end - if you have a discount program, the listed rent should still be the rent due if no rewards are given), when due, in what form it will be paid, discount program details, penalty and late fees, grace periods, bad check fees and any other subject important to you as a landlord regarding any aspect of rent.

* **Deposits:** What do deposits cover? Are they refundable? What actions constitute the loss of those deposits?

* Length of contract (month-to-month, year-long, etc.)

* Allowable uses: Can employees live in your office unit? Can your residential tenant have friends move in? How long can people stay with the tenant before they break the rules?

* Property inclusions: are appliances included with the unit? If so, who is responsible for repair - you or the tenant? Ditto furniture, flooring and the like.

* Nonassignment clause: make it clear the property cannot be sublet.

* Special restrictions: Are pets allowed? Kids? Loud equipment? How many vehicles are permitted at the property?

* Repair policy: Who makes which repairs? What kind of reimbursement is available to tenants? What are the rewards and punishments of the program?

* Maintenance policy: What maintenance is your responsibility? What maintenance is the tenant's responsibility? What rewards or punishments do you offer in this regard?

* Improvement policy: What improvements can the tenant make to the property? If allowed, must all requests and approval be in writing? Can they put in a deck? Do you allow a new paint job (even if it's pink)? Will you reimburse the tenant for his or her work? Will you pay for supplies that lead to increased property value? Who will file the notice of non-responsibility?

* Utilities: Who pays for phone (you may want to require the tenant to have a phone), heat, electricity and water services? Who pays the deposits?

* Inspection: Perform a thorough inspection of the property with the tenant prior to occupancy. Use a checklist that lists everything you can possibly think of. Include defects, appliances included, working condition of appliances and systems. You may even want to include photographs for later comparison. Take the time to make the inspection complete and come to agreement on the unit's condition. This way there can be no dispute later down the line.

* **Legal obligations of the tenant for your property's jurisdiction.** Include relevant local and state laws.

* **Rules and regulations:** Here's your catchall section. Detail what constitutes theft (taking your property off the premises) and what the consequences are if theft occurs. Similarly be clear about your responsibility for the tenant's property (do you require renter's insurance?). Outline what constitutes abandonment of the property (when does a long vacation become abandonment) and what are the consequences of such? Your policy for entering the apartment (written notice or a phone call; how much advance notice will you offer?) in case of emergency and non emergencies, showing the property to prospective new tenants, etc.

Have your attorney go over the document with you for legality and enforceability. Have him or her also advise you as to what additional clauses you need for your protection. Disclosure of landlord/agent, validity of the contract, full disclosure, severability clause, holdover tenancy clause, disaster clause, waivers and the like are important to have in the contract.

Along with the rental contract, you may want to have the tenant sign other documents that can be attached. Consent for maintaining a pet gives the details about what kind of pet, how big, what extra fees and deposits are expected, rules of conduct for the pet and responsibility for damages. Disclaimer letters can ensure you are not liable for repairs performed by tenants. Any part of the contract that you feel needs to be emphasized and detailed, go ahead and add as an attachment.

However, don't bother with clauses taking away a tenant's right to summary process or making the tenant responsible for major repairs (such as a roof) or clauses that give you the right to the tenant's personal property in lieu of rent (unless a court approves such action) or that terminate the contract if the tenant files for bankruptcy. These sorts of clauses are illegal.

Get everything in the contract you possibly can. A 10-page rental contract is not unreasonable as long as it is to the point. It will take more time to adequately explain every line of your agreement, but taking the time to be sure everyone understands their obligations is a lot easier than trying to fix the relationship once it's broken. You think it's time-consuming to explain the contract, try evicting an angry tenant who feels he or she is in the right.

You can always change the contract down the road when it is time for renewal. And a properly drafted rental agreement will allow you to make changes (including raising the rent) when it is necessary to do so.

A rental agreement automatically renews each month unless one of the parties cancels it. And changes, as well as cancellations, need to be in writing and with proper notice (usually 30 days for rental agreements). Leases automatically terminate at the end of the stated term. They are only renewed if both parties agree and, in the case of any lease over one year in length, the agreement is in writing. You can set it up within the lease's language that the lease can be terminated with 60 days notice, but, to some degree, that defeats the advantage of a lease over a rental agreement by basically turning the lease into a 60-day rental agreement.

There are many fill-in-the-blank rental contract forms available, but with the wide range of properties out there and the variety of management styles available, you are best served by developing a rental contract unique to your needs and in accordance with local rules, regulations and custom.

Rent

You may choose to let tenants decide the due date for their rent. If you own just a few small properties, this shouldn't be a problem. However, if your operation is large, such an allowance may not be feasible. If you set no due date in the rental contract, many states will set one for you. Most states will also have rules requiring that when the due date falls on a weekend or holiday it will automatically be extended to the next business day. You should still have this set out in the contract. Some states also have rules as to late charges - some mandate grace periods, some mandate whether or not such charges need to be written into the contract, others cap percentages or disallow them altogether. Be aware of the rules in your state and cover all your bases by spelling out your rules in the contract.

No matter what your policy (late fee charged after four days, eviction after ten days, whatever you decide within the restraints of the law), put it in the contract and be consistent. Even if the tenant has a good reason for being late and you have no intention of charging him or her a late fee or beginning eviction proceedings, you should send a written notice to the tenant as soon as the due date passes. You may need this paper trail later.

Many tenants don't move in on their rental due date, so you will have to develop a policy for prorating the rent. The most simple and fair way is to figure out how much the tenant would pay per day if he or she were renting the unit for the entire month (divide the rent amount by the number of days in the month) then charge the tenant only for those days he or she will be renting the unit (multiply the amount per day by the number of days the tenant will be in residence).

The rental contract should also set out your preferred mode of rent collection, including to whom the rent is to be paid (you or your representative). Do you want tenants to mail you the rent, drop it by your office or wait for you to come by and collect it? Will you allow bank transfers? Remember, there is an advantage in making it as easy and streamlined as possible for your tenants to pay.

If you choose to have tenants mail you the rent, you may still find yourself having to go to them in case of delays. Depending on the reliability and number of your tenants, you may choose to collect it yourself. Similarly, if you have a limited number of units, having tenants drop off rent can be less than ideal. If you have a rental office on the premises, then this is no problem.

If you decide to go out and collect your rent in person, don't go alone. You never know who might be watching and noticing your routines. Don't be a target for thieves. The upside of collecting the rent in person is that it allows you to keep in personal contact with your tenants and your property. The downside is that it is time-consuming and it gives tenants the perfect opportunity to complain.

Just as with other regulations regarding rent, if you don't set it up in the rental contract, some states make the decision for you.

Will you or your representative accept cash, checks, money orders or credit cards for rental payment? In most situations, all are appropriate. However, you may want to consider whether or not to accept cash, especially if you are collecting the rent in person. Don't make yourself a target. Tenants will sometimes complain when the cash option is taken away from them. Some don't have bank accounts and will be forced to purchase money orders. But stick to your guns. Cash gives some tenants the chance to argue that the missing $20 was in an envelope when it was dropped off. Cash gives too many the temptation to do things they shouldn't.

When it comes to checks, don't accept post-dated payment. The post-date makes the check a promissory note which could affect eviction proceedings, in essence putting them off until at least the date on the check.

Are you willing to set up and accept bank transfers? It might be easy for your tenants to simply have the rent deducted from their account and put into your account each month. Then all you do is check the account to make sure the rent has been paid. You might also set up a collection account whereby tenants deposit rent money and then your mortgage, taxes and insurance are paid from the account.

Always give the tenant a receipt (those carbon duplicate receipt books are quite handy) that includes the date, the tenant's name, address of the unit, amount paid, amount owed and any balance.

You may designate someone else (such as a property manager) to collect the rent, but be careful. Don't allow him or her to take cash. Be sure the account into which the money is deposited in is in your name and that your signature must be on all checks. Never delegate check-signing authority. Simply speaking, you are removing temptation from before your employees or consultants and making life easier for you and them.

Your rent collection policies drive much of your cash flow. You need the rent payments to pay the mortgage and fund your operation. Be strict. One exception can lead to a whole avalanche of exceptions and soon you are at your tenant's mercy. Put into the rental contract all the unpleasant, costly steps your tenant will have to endure if rent is not paid on time. Then put all those nasty little steps into action just as promised.

Don't be intimidated by tenant complaints about your tough policy. After all, if the tenant pays the rent on time there will be nothing to ever complain about. Be wary of tenants who are overly concerned about your late payment policies.

It is always simpler to raise the rent in small increments rather than in large ones. Most tenants will complain of double-digit increases even if the rent has remained unchanged for several years, but most will understand a single-digit increase each year. Figuring out how much and how often to raise rents can be as much an art as a science. You want to make a profit so you raise the rent. But if you raise it too far or too often you run the risk of alienating and losing tenants. Be careful; don't get greedy.

Even if you have a lease that mandates rent increases, it is still best to send the tenant advance notice (usually 30 days). Some states have laws as to how much notice you must give, regardless of the specific type of contract you are using. With the shorter term rental agreement, you have the flexibility of raising the rent any month (though notice is still advised). It is again that tenant stability versus rent increase flexibility dilemma.

As always, be consistent. Raise everyone's rent, not just one tenant's. The appearance of discrimination can be just as damning as the existence of discrimination in the eyes of the law.

Rent Control

Rent control (aka: statutory tenancy) stabilizes or prevents rental increases and can affect your management, including how you deal with security deposits and evictions. It began in the 1940s because of World War II housing shortages. It began as a widespread edict by the federal government and evolved into rules imposed by various localities. Designed to protect the poor, rent control is now the privilege of the lucky. There are no rules as to who is eligible to rent a controlled unit. Rich, poor or in between, any tenant lucky enough to find a rent-controlled unit may benefit from the regulations. They may even sublet the unit at a considerably higher rate and keep the difference for themselves.

In some cases, the landlord has the right to raise the rents when one tenant leaves and another moves in. In other cases, the controlled rental unit can be passed on to a family member (with some restrictions). Eviction in rent control areas is complicated and difficult. Know the rules of your area.

Rent control boards (some elected, some appointed) regulate the controlled areas. The board interprets ordinances and some may approve or disapproval landlord requests to increase rent. They can even levy penalties and mandate what changes may be made to your property.

Currently, only Maryland, New York, New Jersey, California and the District of Columbia use rent control in areas. However, there is no guarantee that it will stay this way. Rent control can pollinate anywhere. To protect your property and your income stream know which way the political winds are blowing in your local area.

Many areas are phasing out rent control through a process known as vacancy decontrol. Through this process, rent is slowly raised as tenants move out, are evicted or when leases are renewed. However, the process can take years.

Lease Options and Equity-Sharing

A lease option can be a nice way to get the tenant to pay for maintenance. By giving the tenant the option of eventually buying the property, you are giving him or her a privilege. In exchange the tenant usually pays a fee (nonrefundable and not taxable until the option is exercised) or a higher rent and begins to care for the property as if they are the homeowner (but without the benefits of title or equity). Until the tenant exercises the option and purchases the property (and a good number won't) you keep the title and equity, and lose the hassle of maintenance.

Equity-sharing is similar to a lease option in that you give someone else part of the ownership to eliminate negative cash-flow. You may share equity with a tenant or an investment partner, but either way you are taking on a partner. The difference is whether or not that partner occupies the property.

The partner pays all the property payments and gets benefits of half-ownership - tax write-offs and appreciation. Though a resident partner will be paying higher rent, the tax advantages may mean he or she still ends up saving money. Many tenants will appreciate just the simple opportunity to own (even if only half) property with no down payment and without going through the loan application process. Of course, you'd best make sure this person is the one with whom you want to share property ownership. Because having the tenant be half-owner of the property complicates pretty much every level of the landlord-tenant relationship.

If you attract an investor who will pay the mortgage in exchange for partial ownership, you sidestep a lot of the landlord-tenant complications inherent in the above scenario. But you are still stuck with a partner.

The equity-sharing contract should have a set time limit. Both you and your co-owner need to know when you can cash in on all that equity. How long you stay co-owners is up to the two of you, but get it in writing. At the end of that period, one of you can buy out the other or you can sell the property and split the profits.

Dealing with Inherited Tenants

There are pros and cons to inheriting tenants when you buy a rental property. Yes, you don't have to go through all the trouble of advertising your property and interviewing applicants and preparing the unit for viewing. However, neither do you have the level of comfort of knowing your tenants and having the confidence that they are the tenants you would have chosen. Choosing tenants can be extremely personal. After all, you are looking for people who fit in with your vision of your property, your management style and possibly the other tenants whom you did choose.

When you were going through the buying process, you got some information through estoppel certificates and various copies on the current tenants and their leases. However, things may have changed, information may have been incomplete and you'll want to meet with and hear from tenants yourself. A good way to get to know your tenants is to stop by and visit. But before you pop in, give the tenant adequate notice. Let each know who you are, how they can reach you, where they can find you and when, your expectations regarding rental payments and maintenance. Also reassure them that they do not have to pay new security deposits. Put all this information in a letter along with when you would like to meet them face-to-face. This way tenants can get familiar with your policies before meeting with you so they have time to prepare questions. This is also a good chance to go around and make sure that all your keys work. If a tenant has changed a lock, get a duplicate, explaining to them that you need it in case of emergency and that without it they will be held liable for damages.

When you meet with tenants, be prepared to talk about yourself and your history. Take the time to answer questions. You want to present yourself as an authority figure but not a dictator. After all, you will be eventually negotiating new leases with these tenants and you don't want to go into those proceedings with a hostile adversary. You also don't want to risk losing tenants early in your business when positive cash flow is a must.

Use these meetings to get to know the tenants as well. Get a copy of any leases or rental agreements. Ask about tenants' jobs and families. Leave a form (with self-addressed envelope) that tenants can return, detailing much of the information you would want in a rental application and that you will need at lease renewal/renegotiation time: name, addresses, phone numbers, number of people in the unit (plus their names, relationship, etc), any pets (species, size, etc.) and emergency contacts. If tenants choose, let them fill the forms out on the spot.

Give the tenants some time (a week or two) to return the forms, then follow up if they don't. Explain that you are not trying to be a hardcase, but that this information is mutually beneficial for you and them. Reassure them that you will keep the information confidential.

By the time you close on a property, you should know what deposits and fees current tenants have made and how they are escrowed. Make sure deposits and fees are transferred into your account. You will have to live up to all rental contracts you that are in place when you buy real estate. This includes returning deposits as set out in those agreements. If the previous owners spent those deposits, you will have to either pay them yourself or take the owner to court to recapture them. They are still your responsibility.

Complaints and Disputes

Can't we all just get along? Not likely. There are almost always complaints. But some you can avoid by carefully and firmly explaining and enforcing your rules. Good communication can head off misunderstandings. Misunderstandings often lead to complaints. Complains easily become disputes. Be clear in all your communications with tenants. Tell tenants what you will do, not what you are considering. Give yes or no answers whenever possible.

Keep in mind that although you are the manager, tenants are not your employees. Tenants are your customers. Treat them as such. Be prompt and courteous responding to tenant complaints and requests. And keep your promises. Don't make your tenant repeatedly ask you to do something you said you would. That will only irritate the tenant and in turn irritate you. Try to keep communications civil and unemotional. Remember, this is a business.

When you repair something, save yourself time and energy by doing it right the first time. Short-term budget and time restraints often lead to shoddy workmanship. Resist the temptation. It'll only cost you more in the long run.

You can't evict a tenant for disagreeing with you. You can't even give the impression that that is what you are doing. Some states have laws that assume you are retaliating if you evict a tenant within a specified time period after a tenant lodges a complaint. Find out the laws in your state and remember that the weight of the law usually comes down on the side of the party with the least power - in your case, the tenant.

Some disputes will take more than your goodwill to solve. So always keep a paper trail. Before and after pictures of repairs are a good idea as well, especially when it comes to housing code violations. Keep maintenance and repair logs for all you do and note when complaints come in and how and when they are handled. It is best to include a clause in your rental contracts requiring all complaints to be made in writing.

Now, not all complaints and disputes will even involve you. Tenants won't always get along with each other and you may be the first to hear about it. Many tenants find it easier to go to the landlord with complaints than to the person with whom they have the complaints (just as they may rather go to an inspector with a complaint about the property before they go to you). Of course, you can't do much more about the dispute than the tenants themselves. You can talk to the tenant about whom you've received a complaint, but that's about it. If a tenant's dog is barking, you can't go in the unit and calm the animal, even if you get along great with the dog and the tenant - not without permission. It is best in these situations to advise the tenant bringing the complaint that all you can do is talk to his or her adversary. If that doesn't work, the tenant can always call the police or other officials.

Tenants can (and do) intentionally damage property and then report the damage to authorities in order to get out of rent and/or eviction. There's not a lot you can do in these situations except keep good records and make repairs as quickly as possible with follow-up inspections to prove you are a good landlord. Whatever you do, remain calm, especially if you end up in court. Let the tenant rant and rave and go off on accusatory tangents. You keep your cool and be professional at all times. Let cooler heads prevail.

Eviction

Landlords don't evict people because it's fun. They evict because rental investment is a business. And a business needs to make money if it is to survive. A rental unit that doesn't bring in money is a financial liability. Eviction should never be personal and should never be begun for any other reason than the money - either the tenant is not paying the rent or the tenant is costing you money by being a nuisance (breaking the lease or rental agreement) and affecting other areas of your business (such as destroying property or causing other renters in the unit to leave). You need to get the unit back into a positive cash flow. Sometimes the only way to do this is to get rid of the current tenant and get in a new one - one that pays the rent and doesn't cost you.

You may choose eviction for other reasons, such as wanting the unit for a friend or family member, but this is not a business decision. This is a personal decision and you need to think carefully about it. Do you really want to be in the position of being landlord to a friend or family member? Putting yourself into a power position in a personal relationship can be poisonous. What happens if your friend doesn't pay the rent or damages the property or causes problems with other tenants? You could end up losing not only money but the relationship. Be careful.

Eviction (the termination of tenancy) is never easy. In fact it is likely to be the absolute worst part of your job. Not just because it can be a complicated process, but also because you will often get to know your tenants. No matter how business-minded you are, there is still the knowledge that you are kicking a person out of his or her home. It is especially tough when the tenant is someone you like with legitimate reasons for not being able to pay you rent. But exceptions set precedents. And precedents can undermine your entire program.

The process is designed to protect the tenant. And well it should be. Taking a person's home is serious business. You can't evict because you're mad that the tenant called the housing authority on you, nor can you evict because the tenant joined a tenant organization. In fact, if you do evict soon after such events, some states will automatically assume it is retaliation and go after you. Just keep your emotions out of your business and you will be a better landlord.

For the most part, evictions happen in two steps: a written notice of termination (often called a notice to quit) informing the tenant that he or she has to either leave the unit or fix the problem or else. The second step is the "or else" part of the process. If nothing happens after the notice, you file an eviction lawsuit and have the tenant removed from your property. This removal comes after court proceedings and does not happen with you grabbing the tenant by the back of the neck. The physical removal needs to be done by a court-recognized authority (sheriff, police officer, etc.).

Sound simple? It's not. Nothing in the legal system ever is. There will be summonses, court dates, evidence, agreements, a judgment, etc. And none of it is necessarily consistent state-to-state. (For a summary of state eviction laws visit www.successdna.com.)

All states have laws to protect tenants and to control how an eviction is performed. However, these laws are not the same every-where, so be sure you know which apply to you and consider using an attorney. Mistakes in handling the process can be costly - much more costly than attorney fees.

Evictions are a hassle. But you don't want to keep bad ten-ants who cost you money. Never fear; there are alternatives. Just as there are fifty ways to leave a lover, there are several ways to get rid of a tenant. One common alternative is to simply pay the tenant to leave. Get on the bus, Gus. Cut a check, give back the security deposit, however you want to do it. Just cut your losses and get the unit back on the market. Of course, this isn't what you want to do. It feels like rewarding the tenant for bad behavior. It's not fair. But it's not about fairness here; it's about money. It's about turning negative cash flow into positive.

Vacancies

For all your efforts at keeping your tenants satisfied, some will leave. That can be good or bad. On the one hand, it may be eas-ier to change rental terms, including increases, when there is no previous history with a tenant. Vacancies also give you the opportu-nity to improve the property (making it even more profitable). On the other hand, vacancies mean cleaning up the unit and fixing all those little things that can easily slide during a tenancy. At a minimum, you're probably looking at new paint, carpet care and seriously thor-ough cleaning. You will have to pay for this sort of sprucing up, while at the same time bringing in no income for the unit.

You may choose to get the unit ready for rental on your own or hire someone to do it for you. Take the quickest route. You may want to hire experienced professionals the first few times and watch how they do it before trying it yourself. Speed is the key because you want to get the unit rented as soon as possible so you have some income coming in again.

To what extremes do you need to go to prepare a unit for rent? Simple, at the least (the very least) the unit should be in the same condition you would expect if you were renting it. Remember that you set the level of respect the tenant will have for the property. If renters are shown a unit that is in ill-repair and in less than clean conditions, they will see that you have no respect for your own property. If they move in, they will carry that same lack of respect and you will likely find yourself with an even bigger cleanup (and repair) job when they move out. If you choose the quick and dirty property preparation, get used to your rents decreasing. A clean, well-functioning unit will always attract a higher rent than one that seems unkempt and downtrodden.

Older buildings will almost always take more work than newer ones. Keeping them looking good takes effort. Keeping up with upgrades takes money. But there are also environmental hazards. Lead paint, asbestos - these were once standards in building. Now they are environmental hazards which can be expensive to remediate. When you are checking laws (and there are many) involved with real estate in your area, don't forget to check the environmental laws. Your local health department should be able to tell you what you need to know when it comes to such hazards.

Fair Housing Laws

There are federal and state fair housing laws. State laws may be more detailed than federal, so be sure to check what antidiscrimination laws pertain to your property. The federal laws you need to be aware of are the Fair Housing Acts (42 U.S.C. 3601-3619 et seq.) and they apply to every state in the union. Under the Act you cannot discriminate against anyone on the basis of age, race (and color), national origin, religion, family status, sex (that means sexual harassment as well) and handicap or disability (current or in the past and including physical or mental disabilities, AIDS or alcoholism if it's being treated or even a person who is seen by others as having a disability). However, in the case of age there are exceptions. Communities for tenants 62 years or older and those for tenants 55 years or older are allowed. In the case of communities for those 55 or older, 80 percent or more of the units have to have at least one person in that age group living in the unit.

There are other exemptions to the Act as well. Some sorts of religious organizations and private clubs can set up tenancy or membership for their own members. Single-family residential units are exempted if rented without using discrimination in the advertising and without using a broker. Owner-occupied buildings with four or fewer rental units are also exempt from the Act.

The Act says you can't discriminate. What exactly does that mean? Well, you can't advertise for just one group (women-only for example), nor can you deny rental to a person based on any of the categories listed above (that includes lying to the person and saying a unit is rented when it's not). You can't have different policies for different tenants (everyone gets the same credit checks, the same background check), nor can you offer different services to different tenants (everyone gets their sink fixed). And, of course, you can't evict someone just because you don't like the group of which they are a member.

However, discrimination can be much more subtle than the examples given above. And it doesn't need to be intentional. The best intentions can dip into discrimination. A lot of problems arise in the wording and even language of ads. Say your property is in a neighborhood where most people speak Japanese. You might think you're going against discrimination by advertising just in Japanese. Wrong, English-speaking people can claim discrimination. English is the only safe language for ads and rental contracts.

Similarly, you can't ask one group of people for proof of citizenship as identification and not others. In fact, you can't require all tenants be citizens of the United States.

You can't refuse occupancy to qualified tenants with kids, or conversely set up your property as family-only. The only way you can limit how many people live in a unit is by enforcing building, housing or health codes or by showing that the property itself limits occupancy (such as with a small septic unit). Otherwise you may be seen as discriminating against families.

When it comes to mental illness, you can't discriminate, but if the person is a danger to others or your property (a background check might pick this up). You must have knowledge of specific instances that back up this danger. You can't just think the tenant seems dangerous. Nor can you ask an applicant if he or she has a disability. And you must show all available units to all applicants regardless if the unit is handicap accessible or not.

Once a tenant moves in you will have to make reasonable renovations to the unit (including perhaps a ramp, appliance modifications and hearing detectors designed for those who are deaf) for accessibility anyway. You may also be required to allow a service dog and read all your communications to a tenant who is blind. You are allowed to request proof that the requested modifications are necessary.

Penalties for discrimination can range from your being forced to rent to the person against whom you discriminated to a wide range of monetary penalties.

Customer Service

We've spent a lot of time here talking about what to do with bad tenants, but spending all your effort on the squeaky wheel can be counterproductive. You never want a good tenant to feel as if he or she is taken for granted. You want the good tenants to stay and give your property and your business stability. Your program will be most effective if it offers not only punishment for bad behavior, but rewards for good behavior as well.

You may choose to forego some profit in favor of stability by not raising rent as quickly with good tenants as with others. You can offer a discount rent to the good tenants who always pay on time. You should always quickly respond to their complaints and always maintain the property in peak condition.

Let the good tenants know how much you appreciate them.

A simple letter filled with your appreciation and compliments that at the same time explains why you must raise the rent goes a long way. From the rental contract stage, your tenants should know that the rent must be increased each year to keep up with increasing costs, but the letter informing them of how much each year should not be dry and impersonal. Let it glow with your esteem and make the tenant feel good about living in their home.

You might also think of a way to celebrate a renter's anniversary with you. Perhaps a one-time discount in the rent or a gift certificate for a dinner or delivery of a gift basket. The little ways you tell a tenant you care can be much more important than the money you ask of them. After all, all landlords ask for money. You can engender loyalty by being different from the others. Loyalty means stability, but it also increases the likelihood of your tenant taking better care of you property and living up to your esteem.

Chapter 16
Money Matters

     Odds are you began your rental investment business to make money. But there's a whole lot more to making money than cashing the checks. You may get the best deal on the property, find the perfect tenants who always pay their rent on time and in full, keep the building in fabulous condition and still find yourself broke in a year. If you don't track the money, you really can't make money.

     Making a profit in real estate takes constant vigilance. You must always know what is coming in as well as what is going out. Recordkeeping should be one of your highest priorities. Don't let it pile up and get out of control. Your best bet is to make time on a regular basis for your records. Or hire it out. There are plenty of good accountants and bookkeepers out there who know how to keep you organized.

Bookkeeping

     Whenever and wherever possible, separate your business life from your personal life. Don't do business in your own name. It is best to hold real estate in a protected entity such as a limited liability company or a limited partnership. As soon as you begin your business, open a separate checking account in the business name of the protective entity you use. If you have multiple properties, you may use one account or a separate one for each property; it's your choice; just be consistent and careful with the details.

     After you set up your checking account, consider short-term and long-term escrow accounts for the paying out of expenses. The short-term account is for regular bills you can anticipate coming due every month, every quarter, etc. (taxes, insurance, utilities, maintenance, supplies and the like). The long-term account is more of an insurance against those big bills that always seem to hit when you can least afford it (new roof, blown furnace, faulty stairs, etc.).

If you are a novice bookkeeper or just don't have the time for it, you may want to consider utilizing a bookkeeping service. As previously mentioned, a good choice is Sierra Financial Center, LLC, a firm that handles real estate bookkeeping for property owners around the country. They can be reached at www.sierrafi.com or by calling 1-775-782-0804.

Knowing how to use a spreadsheet might be enough if you have few tenants and plan to do your own bookkeeping. The program should allow you to enter data and then display it in a variety of ways. If you have more than a few tenants, you will want to look into a bookkeeping program. There area variety of good ones on the market, so take a little time to see which one will work best for you.

Track your rent by address, tenant, due date, amount paid, amount owed, late fees assessed, receipt number and/or any other category to which you routinely look for the status of payments.

You will want to have pertinent property information in one place, whether on paper or in your computer. The following is the sort of information to keep together:

* Property address
* Property legal description and assessor parcel number
* Size of unit
* Owner
* Loans (including interest rates, monthly payments and who holds the loan)
* Insurance (name of insurance company, mailing address, toll free number, as well as the name, address and phone number of your local agent)
* Real estate agent (if you used one, include the name, address and phone number of the agent)
* Taxes (parcel number, tax code number, payments and how made - yearly, part of monthly payments, etc.)

* Valuations of the land and improvements by the assessor
* Lender statements regarding loan status (due date, how much owed, interest rate, terms, amortization table for the loan life)

Give all this information a label (often the address) that can be used with all your other bookkeeping. This label will be the starting point for you financial spreadsheets, wherein you will include all financial transactions for that property. Cross referencing accounts through a label system will simplify your systems while improving your efficiency.

Next, you will want a spreadsheet that sets out all pertinent information on your rental of the property, including:

* Property information code
* Address
* Tenant (name, phone and/or fax numbers, e-mail address, physical address to send correspondence if not the unit address)
* Rental contract start date
* Rental contract end date
* Rental contract renewal options
* Amount of rent increase
* Rent increase date
* Notes

This information, along with the rent status information and the property information will allow you to create a variety of spreadsheets to tell you where you are financially and where you are going.

For expenses, it's a good idea to have a code system for common items such as: mortgage payments, taxes, fire insurance, carpentry, electrical, plumbing and on and on. Your codes can be simple numbers, letters or any combination of the two that works for you.

You may want a separate accounting system or you may find

one system for your bookkeeping and accounting. However, any accounting system you adopt should be a double-entry system. With such, every transaction has two side, two entries - debits and credits. Balancing the books entails making sure that every entry on one side of the ledger has a counterpart on the other side of the column. For example, rent is a credit as it comes in, then becomes a debit as you deposit it in the bank.

Double-entry accounting may seem more time consuming in the beginning, but the first time you find a discrepancy in your books, the first time you have to go back and figure out where an amount of money went, you will be happy you took the time to set it up right. Such systems allow you to check for balances with a glance.

The reports issued from double-entry bookkeeping (such as trial balances, earnings statements, financial statements an comparison reports) are the accepted standard throughout the world. These are the data you will want for tax season. Get your accountant's advice on which programs work best and then have him or her help you set up the most efficient system for your needs. Getting the accountant's advice at the beginning will make his or her job easier, so few accountants mind taking the time to offer this advice.

You need to keep good records of all aspects of your business. Detailed reports of the property and the tenants will go hand-in-hand with spreadsheets listing expenses and income to keep you on top of your responsibilities and to track your profit. Put as much expense detail in these spreadsheets as you can. Tenants have the right to know what your operating costs are annually. You will need to have a system that is easily understood and that substantiates your claims of expenses. Good numbers will help you explain rent increases in ways that all the words in the world can't.

Keep records of the not-so-obvious money categories as well. You should always know how quickly (or slowly) a property is appreciating (or depreciating) and, correspondingly, at what rate rents are changing. Track what it costs to maintain the building as well as the vacancy rate. But you will also have to take into account your time and energy.

You may choose to hire a CPA just during tax season or you

might hire a bookkeeper and/or accountant to take care of the ongoing record-keeping. However you decide to accomplish the task of
recording the numbers and details of your business, be sure that
you are familiar with every aspect of the system. Consultants and
employees come and go, and you don't want your business to end
up in chaos just because of a personnel change.

Never abdicate any portion of your authority to those you hire
to help you. Employees and consultants should help you run your
business, not run the business themselves. You should always be
aware of the day-to-day activities performed on behalf of you and
your business. You should be in regular, consistent contact with any
employee or consultant working for you so that if that relationship
ends, there will be no lapse in the quality of your business endeavors.

Get a filing cabinet. Even if you only have one property, one
tenant, get a filing cabinet. You will need to keep copies of every
piece of paper that comes across your desk in regard to your property - rental applications, credit checks, rental contracts, inspection
checklists, receipts, warnings, complaints, photographs, phone
logs, notes, bills, insurance policies, bank statements - if it killed a
tree, file it.

Deposits and Fees

Security and cleaning deposits are not free cash. Tenants put
down deposits with the understanding that they will get such money
back if rent is paid on time and in full and the unit is not damaged.
Some states limit how much you can require for a security deposit;
some states don't. Again, know the local laws. In general, you
should charge as much as is allowed to ensure you will be able to
recoup your costs for unpaid rent or repairs and to encourage the
tenant to take good care of your property.

Deposits are your insurance against damage to your property and are typically held for such things as: cleaning, stolen property, property damage and/or unpaid rent. The deposit may sometimes be held for unpaid utility bills as well. It depends on local laws.

However, the deposit money cannot be used without notifying the tenant in writing, including the amount of the original deposit, the interest due, an itemized list of how much was taken out (for unpaid rent or to cover damages, repairs, cleaning or missing property) and how much the tenant is owed (or the landlord, depending on the case). Include a check if the tenant is owed money. Even if the tenant is not entitled to the return of any of the deposit, you still need to send the letter explaining why the deposit is not being returned. And the letter needs to be sent out in a timely fashion (how timely is up to the states in which you are doing business).

You cannot deduct costs for normal wear and tear. Of course, what is considered normal is a little tricky. But basically, you should know that paint gets dingy and carpets get dirty. The tenant has a right to inspect the unit and protest your deductions in writing (within a specific amount of time). Be conservative in your deductions and save yourself the hassle of being taken to small claims court.

If the hold back is for unpaid rent, you can't take out the money until this notification and after the tenant is out of the unit. If it is for damage, go ahead and take the money out of the deposit, but be sure to have the tenant repay that amount back into the deposit account.

If you decide to use the deposit to cover the last month's rent (at the tenant's request) make sure you do a thorough inspection of the unit first to be sure you won't need the money to clean up or repair the property or to replace stolen items.

You may choose to collect money for the last month's rent as well. Know your local laws. Some states allow you to use the money as you would a security deposit - for cleaning and repairs. Some states are very strict about keeping these separate. Once you are sure you understand the rules yourself (which should be long before you ever have a tenant sign a rental contract), be sure it is dealt with clearly in the lease or rental agreement.

Some states require the deposit escrow account be held in the landlord and the tenant's name together. Though that sounds complicated, do not worry, the banks in those states will know how to set up the account. Most states will allow one deposit account, but will also require very careful records. Whether interest on deposit monies is due back the tenant will be governed by state law.

Your local state law may also regulate how much you can charge for the deposit as well as how (and how quickly) the money should be returned.

Deposits are meant to protect your property from damage. In order to assess such damage, you need to know what condition the unit was in before the tenant moved in. The checklist you used when examining the property before buying it is a good place to start. Bring out that list and then update it. Go through the property with the tenant, checking items as being in good condition or needing work. For any item that needs work, list what work it needs (does a cupboard need a new handle? The sink a new faucet? Is there a hole behind in the wall where the doorknob hits in the bathroom?). You should also note serial numbers on appliances and don't forget to check the outside of the property, yard, parking lot, etc. Again, some landlords are using video or digital cameras with date notations to record the condition of the property.

Coming to an agreement on unit condition now will save you arguments later. A photographic log of contents and conditions is a nice backup as well.

Have the tenant sign an agreement listing the names of all parties involved, phone numbers and address. Let the agreement state the amount of deposit, whether or not the deposit is refundable and under what terms. Have the tenant sign it and sign it yourself with the date. It's always good to have proof that everyone understands the agreement.

After the tenant moves out you will repeat the inspection to assess any damage. You may perform this inspection with the tenant (several states give the tenant the right to accompany you during the inspection) or by yourself. Having the tenant present allows you to explain why you are keeping all or part of the deposit - a discussion you may or may not want to have. Photographs are again recommended for your records. It is also advisable to bring along a witness for the inspection, just in case you end up in court.

To ensure the deposit money can actually be accessed if the tenant reneges on the agreement and you need that money, insist that it be paid only in cash, money order or a non-cancelable cashier's check. Another option might be taking possession of valuable personal property (such as title to a car) in lieu of the deposit. If you choose this option, make sure the agreement is very specific and lists all terms, including who is exchanging what for how much of a deposit, whether or not cash can be exchanged later for return of the item, details of the item (serial number or the like), signatures and date.

If damages do occur, and if you did allow for a security deposit in your rental contract, you should be able to keep that money for repairs. However, if the damage costs more to fix than you have in deposit money, your best response is likely to just let it go. It will probably cost more in time and money to try and collect than it is worth.

Other fees routinely charged by landlords include:

* **Pet deposits:** Money used to insure specifically against damages done by a pet (usually a dog or cat). This fee is usually refundable.

* **Credit check processing fees:** Landlords pay a fee for credit checks and can pass that fee on to the tenant. This fee is seldom refundable.

* **Holding fee:** A tenant may put down money for a right of first refusal on a unit. If the tenant chooses to rent the unit within a specified amount of time, the fee is usually refundable.

As usual, laws regarding refundable and non-refundable fees vary state to state. It is always your responsibility to know the laws that apply to your property and your business. Violation of these laws may not be a minor issue. They can run several times the amount of the original deposit or fees. Be careful.

Expenses

There are two primary ways to increase profits in rental property management: 1) more rent and 2) fewer expenses.

Some common expenses for rental properties include:

vacancy, management, maintenance supplies (light bulbs, cleaning supplies and equipment, construction materials), advertising, utilities (gas/oil/propane/electric, water, sewer), garbage collection, basic maintenance, taxes, insurance and professional consulting fees (accountant, lawyer). Depending on the type of property (residential vs. commercial) and its location, you might also be looking at janitorial, window washing, elevator maintenance, parking lot cleanup, landscape upkeep, even snow removal. You will have to decide how much to spend on each expense and whether or not you will be the one doing the spending. Some, if not all, these types of expenses can be passed onto the tenant.

There are many ways to cut expenses. Be creative when you look at the books with an eye toward saving money. Don't overlook the little things. For example, if you pay for garbage service, have only one can per unit. Some tenants expect two, but how many of us really need two cans when we have weekly garbage pickup? If a tenant insists on a second, explain that it is not your policy, but you'd be happy to change the rental contract so that they pay for that second can.

Another cost-cutting measure is to maintain control over utilities in common areas. Don't let tenants have access to thermostats or lights in common areas. If you pay the bill, you should be in charge of the utilities. Teaching tenants a thing or two about conservation (turning lights off when they leave a room and that sort of thing) will help as well. A few well-placed signs (such as in restrooms) can be a good reminder.

However, in both the examples used above it would be even more cost-effective to make tenants pay for their own utility and garbage service. These expenses go up every year and you have no control over how much. It is simpler to put the tenant in charge rather than have to recalculate rent based on these increases each year (let alone the hassle of raising the rent more and more each year to cover the rising costs). Let the utility and garbage companies explain to tenants why their fees are increasing. Property improvement loans are available from the Department of Housing and Urban Development to cover costs of such undertakings as converting central heating, cooling and electrical meters to individual units. In most every case, the savings will be worth the costs of converting.

You might consider hiring and/or training a super (short for superintendent). Yes, the super will already know the ins and outs of repair, but you will need to train him or her in the rules and expectations of your program.

Some issues to consider are:

* Are tenants expected to make small repairs themselves? Then the super will need to know how and when to tell tenants to fix it on their own.
* Do you want the super using used parts when feasible?
* Do you expect the super to get several estimates on jobs that need to be contracted out?
* Will the super be expected to coordinate and supervise contract help?
* At what level of cost do you expect the super to get your approval before making a repair?
* What time line do you expect him of her to work under? Do you expect all repairs to be made within a week of the first complaint? A month?
* Do you expect the super to be proactive when he or she sees items needing repair?
* Will the super be an employee or contract worker?
* Will you pay the super by the hour or on salary?

A super can save you more money than he or she costs. Having someone familiar with your program and your properties increases the efficiency of operations. Plus it is a lot cheaper to have work done by a super than by say, a professional plumber. Not only will it be a cheaper hourly rate, but the super can and should look for ways to save you money on every repair.

Taxes

Death and taxes - no one gets away. You may take on the

task of filing and payment of taxes yourself or hire it out to a competent tax professional (usually a CPA). But even if you choose to do your taxes yourself, you should find a good tax attorney, real estate attorney or experienced accountant whom you can ask questions. No matter how much you think you know, unless you are a tax professional or have extensive rental management experience, you may be taking a risk when attempting to handle your own taxes.

Whether commercial or residential property, you will be paying property taxes. Property taxes are figured from the assessed value and paid to the municipality and/or county where the property physically sits. Payment is usually broken into four installments a year. Property taxes are your fees for holding the property for the year. Someone has to pay for the schools and roads and services in the area and the local property owners, who hopefully benefit with increased real estate appreciation when such services are efficiently delivered, are the ones to pay.

Insurance

Even more than taxes, insurance is probably the least favorite subject for landlords. After all, at first glance, what do you get in return?

But then look at it this way, people who have totaled their cars don't usually mind paying car insurance. If you ever lost your home in a fire, you appreciate fire insurance. Anyone who had a serious illness understands the need for health insurance. What you get for your insurance payment is peace of mind, but also the assurance that your business can survive the risks and uncertainties of everyday life. You cannot plan for every threat to your business. From natural disaster to human error to plain-old stupidity, it is simply easier to cover your bases and leave the worrying at the door. Besides, most lenders will require the property to be insured if they are going to approve your loan.

As an owner of an existing property, you will need rent replacement insurance with a worker's compensation rider as well as fire and extended coverage. An umbrella override policy is also good protection. If you will be living at the rental property you own, you will also want to have homeowners insurance just as you would on any other property at which you lived. Your lender may also require you to have mortgage insurance to make sure the lender gets paid and title insurance to protect against ownership disputes. If you have employees or others working within your team, you may opt for a master policy naming others as "additional insureds" on your policy. This avoids duplications and can save money for everyone involved.

As a builder, you will need worker's compensation, construction, fire and extended coverage as well as liability umbrella insurance. A master policy in this case could save a whole lot of money. In fact, it could be the deciding factor in making a project being economically feasible.

When it comes to closing fire insurance, there is a difference between replacement value policies and cash value policies. Replacement value policies cover the costs of actually replacing the building at current market costs. A cash value policy means an insurance company sends out an appraiser to determine what the building was worth. If that determination yields a price lower than your insured amount, you only get that appraised amount. If the determination yields a higher price, you only get up to the amount for which you insured the building. But remember, if your property has appreciated a cash value policy may not leave you with enough money to rebuild.

Just as with your car insurance or health insurance, you can choose your deductible. The higher the deductible, the lower the cost of the policy.

For repairs and even maintenance, you will want to be sure that everyone performing such services (including you) carries liability (insurance for injuries suffered by third parties) and workman's compensation insurance (insurance for injuries suffered by people doing work on your property) at a minimum. You may also require consultants to carry errors and omissions insurance or other specialty coverage depending on what services the consultant offers.

You may choose to have tenants carry renter's insurance. Some landlords require that they be named on the policy as well as the renter to protect their investment. Other landlords use part of the rent to cover renter's insurance. Regardless of how you set up your rental contracts, it is a good idea to let tenants know about renter's insurance. Many tenants (especially younger ones) don't know it exists and will be thankful for the information. Others may be surprised at how inexpensive it is or how extensive the coverage can be (even covering property not on the premises). A tenant with renter's insurance is simply less likely to blame you for losses or damages to his or her property if those losses are covered by insurance.

Chapter 17
Maintenance

You've got all your units rented, everyone's paying rent on time and in full, now all you have to do is sit back and count your money, right? Not likely. Even the best building in the best neighborhood with the best tenants will need maintenance.

Keep on top of standard repairs so they don't become the kinds of problems that kill reserves and leave your entire operation vulnerable.

Common repairs include, but are by no means limited to:

* fixing holes in the walls
* putting in new locks
* painting (inside and out)
* installing carpet
* changing washers
* replacing windows and screens
* repairing major appliances (refrigerator, stove, oven, washer, dryer)
* unplugging toilets
* changing fuses
* cleaning common areas
* repairing or replacing broken light fixtures

As with every other aspect of your business, you want to be prepared for routine maintenance. Before you ever collect your first rent check you should have a good idea as to what sorts of skills will be necessary, what skills you possess and what skills you will need to hire out.

Even if you have the skills, will you have the time to do repairs yourself? Could your time be more valuable in other pursuits? Are you regularly available for repairs? If you have a day job or travel a lot, you will need others on call to handle emergency repairs. A tenant with a flooded kitchen doesn't really care who fixes the problem; he or she just wants it fixed. And since tenants are paying you so much of their hard-earned money, they aren't interested in your schedule.

Knowing this, you should have decided whether to hire a super or pay for help as needed by different professionals or one independent contractor. Will you be offering a salary or an hourly contract? Will you require bids on each project or will you defer to a contractor's relationship with you and your property? Either way, you should have a relationship with those who will be working on your building and an agreement as to how repairs will be made and how much they will cost. You don't want to be scrambling around at midnight trying to find a plumber to fix a tenant's busted pipes.

Five percent of the money you collect for rent should be put aside for standard repairs. If you hire a professional as a super or as contract help, you may find he or she is eligible for discounts on equipment and materials. Hiring an independent contractor (as opposed to an employee) will save you money on taxes and may, in some states, also decrease your liability (if your repairs lead to injury, you may be liable). In addition, you won't be paying social security or other taxes and the contractor will have his or her own insurance, equipment and crew.

You want to be aware of the condition of your property more than just at moving time. Some landlords perform twice yearly inspections of the property and plan repairs accordingly. If you leave some maintenance up to the tenant, such as changing furnace filters, it is a good idea to send reminder letters. These letters can remind the tenant that the change is due while listing the steps involved with the repair. The easier you make it, the more likely it is to be done.

You may include janitorial and/or landscaping with maintenance duties or separate them out. If you are dealing with a single-family home rental, you probably don't even need janitorial or landscaping (though you may want to take care of landscaping in order to be sure it gets done and your property values do not go down when the yard is trashed).

But if you have a multiunit rental (residential or commercial), you may find yourself with common areas needing upkeep. If the common area is small, you might take care of it yourself or have your property manager or super keep everything presentable. Or you might hire a janitorial company or allow a tenant to take care of these services in exchange for reduced rent. The choice is yours, of course, but do make the choice.

Don't let common areas get dingy or in disrepair. Common areas are usually the first things potential clients and tenants will see. Remember first impressions. A shabby lobby sends a message that you don't care about the building. If you don't care about the condition of your property, why should a tenant? Set a good example.

Never let repairs or maintenance that contribute to safety go unchecked. Safety should always be a top priority.

Know what laws refer to maintenance and repair of your property. All states have building codes (setting out minimum standards, usually referring to construction, mechanical and electrical details), but housing (dictating safety and sanitary standards), fire (safety and fire prevention issues) or health (environmental and sanitary conditions) codes are quite common as well. Other less common codes that might affect your business include:

* maintenance codes
* blight codes
* historical codes
* resident codes

When your property is not up to code, you can be fined hefty amounts and put yourself at risk for serious liability. The codes are designed to protect your tenants and your property. They are not meant to put undue burden on you. Run a safe property with common sense (if you don't have a license to perform certain duties, you can't perform them, whether you own the property or not) and a bit of forethought (smoke detectors, healthy wiring, etc.) and you will be surprised how little there is to worry about within the codes.

A little preventive maintenance goes a long way. Talk to experts when you buy the property. What steps can you take before renters move in (as well as during their tenancy and after) to decrease maintenance and safety concerns? Use quality products - commercial grade whenever possible. Use doorstops or wall protectors to decrease the occurrence of holes in the wall. Keep smoke detectors (and carbon monoxide filters if you have them - some states require them) in good working condition, including working batteries (or install wired detectors). Calk cracks to keep out moisture (and bugs). Keep rain gutters clean to protect the building's roof and foundation. Use adequate insulation and storm windows to increase efficiency (especially if you are paying utility bills yourself). Make sure floors are properly sealed (especially vinyl and wood floors) to keep out water. All windows and doors should be fully functioning - able to easily open and close - and should have locks.

You always want to give good tenants an incentive to stay with you, so always be thinking service. What services can you add? Commercial enterprises are often looking for the best telephone service they can find. How does your rate? Can you afford an upgrade? Can those costs be passed on to the tenant? Do you have a UPS or FedEx drop box on the property?

What about services you can add that cost nothing? Find a local sandwich or muffin delivery service and ask them to put your building on their route. Put together a folder with menus from local restaurants that deliver to your area. Think about what services would make your day easier and then offer those services to your tenants. Not only will your tenants appreciate this, but the local businesses to whom you give business will think more kindly of you and thus networking begins. They may refer potential tenants back to you.

Renovations are another service you can offer tenants. If you can afford to renovate when you take over, you are sending a signal to tenants that you care about the property and them. You are making their businesses look better. This small token may come in handy when you begin renegotiating rental contracts.

Before you bought the building, you should have gained a thorough understanding of its needs through conversations with the previous owner and your own experience and inspections. With this information, you should be able to set up some sort of schedule for routine maintenance. Have checklists for daily (emptying garbage, vacuuming), weekly (checking light bulbs, mopping), monthly (storage and stocking up of supplies), quarterly (changing filters for heating and cooling systems), season (switching from heating to cooling) and yearly (checking the roof) maintenance duties. In addition, you can furnish janitorial staff or even tenants with a checklist of all foreseeable repairs. As they come due, the janitor or tenant can notify you of the need for repair. Make either (or both) feel comfortable with alerting you to issues before they become problems and get them used to taking care of the little things themselves. For example, supply the janitorial staff or tenants with light bulbs so they can change them when the need arises.

Just because you contract out, doesn't mean you never set foot in the building. For commercial sites, get used to performing monthly maintenance inspections for yourself. You may inspect less frequently if you have a property manager but you will still want to inspect your investment on a periodic basis.

Do whatever is necessary to keep on top of maintenance problem. It is much easier to fix a leaking roof than to replace one. It is far less expensive to fix a leaking sink than replace a floor ruined by water damage.

If you have a single-family unit and you have a rental contract making the tenants responsible for all maintenance and repairs, you should still check in on the property from time to time (with proper notice). It may be their home, but it is your investment. And just because a tenant signs the contract, that doesn't guarantee they will live up to its clauses. You need to know if tenants are performing their responsibilities. If not, you should have the right to make repairs yourself (or contract them out) and charge the tenant (again, after written notification). This fact should be in the signed rental contract.

Being proactive and thorough may seem more time-consuming, but in the end it will save you time and money. The same goes with how repairs are made. Don't keep doing the minimum just to save money. It often costs less to replace an item than it does to repair it a dozen times. This, of course, requires a degree of knowledge. You or your hirees will need to be able to tell when to use duct tape and when to break out the cash.

Environmental Hazards

Beware of lead, asbestos, mold and radon. No words strike fear into an experienced landlord's heart quite like "lead," "asbestos," "mold" and "radon." If you hear those words, start thinking money. Start saying goodbye to your reserves. Obviously, you want to avoid these hazards by doing sufficient research before you even buy the property. Local health agencies can help you figure out how to detect these and other hazards.

Lead used to be part of a lot of construction elements (such as paint, pipes and solder), but has been shown as being a potential cause of learning disabilities in children when consumed. This is an especially big problem in the case of peeling paint. However, encapsulation paints can now be purchased to mediate the problem.

Asbestos was once used as insulation, but its dust has been linked to a cancer. If the dust is found, it must be removed. There is no other abatement. Removal can be expensive and complicated and is best handled by a professional (some states require it).

Mold is the growth of spores in damp areas and in vents. Some tenants may claim their health is affected by the presence of mold. Insurance companies are refusing to cover such claims. You must become very aware of the risks and responsibilities associated with mold in your local market.

Radon is a radioactive gas that has no color, no taste and no color and is associated with lung cancer as well as other illnesses. Radon detectors are currently on the market (results can be tested at a local laboratory) and it is especially important to test older buildings, especially those with poor ventilation.

Reserves

Reserves are accounts you set up for all those "just in case" moments inherent in real estate investment and management. Anyone who has ever owned property knows that when repairs hit suddenly, they can be hit hard. The roof needs fixed, the pipes need upgraded, the utilities need to be expanded, the air conditioner has hit its useful end, a refrigerator needs replaced. And anyone who has ever worked with people knows that such repairs will constitute an emergency for those living with the property - the tenants. So you will, inevitably, be faced with large repairs that need to be taken care of right away. How are you going to fund such emergencies? The best way is through reserves.

Your reserves should also be able to cover your expenses should your property go vacant (or partially so) or if a tenant declares bankruptcy. Having six months worth or mortgage, insurance and tax payments in reserve is a good safety net. You may be unable to find a renter after an eviction or tenant leaving or you may have to leave a unit vacant while making necessary upgrades or repairs. Either way, you never want to find yourself in the position of having to borrow money to make your monthly payments.

Reserves should account for about 10 percent of your budget and should be kept in an account separate from others where it can collect interest while awaiting that "just in case" moment.

Conclusion

Investing in real estate is not an exact science, and therefore has some inherent risks. However, when compared with investing in just about anything else, real estate involves relatively low risk for the simple reason that you can control most elements of a real estate investment. For instance, you have full control over where you invest (areas with measurably and consistently higher growth rates than other areas), when to buy, what to buy, and through which lenders you get your finance. Similarly, you can control which tenants you lease your property to, whether or not to effect improvements on the property, and when (if ever!) you want to sell. Furthermore, real estate is relatively simple to learn (no three-year college course required), easy to practice (you don't need to be certified in any way as a pre-requisite to investing in real estate), and easy to look after (hire a property manager).

Perhaps most importantly from an investment point of view, it is relatively easy to make large amounts of money through investing in real estate, a fact made all the more appealing by the reality that you do not need to have much capital to achieve this. To be sure, there are many people who make obscene amounts of money from such things as stocks (consider Warren Buffet), currencies (George Soros) high-tech (Bill Gates), cars (Henry Ford), fashion (Ralph Lauren), and in a multitude of other endeavors. However, it is our contention, that if you take groups of 1,000 people, all chosen at random, and you train one group to invest in stocks, the next group to invest in currencies, the next in high-tech, the next in automobiles, the next in fashion, as so on, and you also take one group of 1,000 people and train them to invest in real estate, then at the end of 10 years, the real estate investors will on average have greatly outperformed all other investors. Not only will the average performance of the real estate investors be far higher, but the standard deviation in performance will be much lower, meaning that the numbers will not be skewed by one or two hyper-success stories that boost the average but leave the masses to the wills of chance.

The few hazards that there are when it comes to investing in real estate are for the most part easy to overcome. We have shown in this book that by making smart choices with respect to real estate agents, property acquisitions, property management, accounting, tenant selection and general attitude, it is easy to minimize the few risks that there are, and maximize your chances of making money on a scale that few other investments afford.

At no stage did we claim that investing in real estate was exhilarating, captivating, or even mildly exciting. However, by applying the ideas set forth in this book, you can easily build up equity and passive income that enables you to do the things you really do find exhilarating without having to worry about how you are going to pay for it. Now that is exciting.

Glossary

acquisition - acquiring, becoming the owner

ALTA Title Insurance - insurance for protection against all known and unknown defects of title

amortization schedule - installment time schedule for paying off a loan

appreciation - property value increase

asbestos - construction material no longer used that causes respiratory diseases

Assessor - County employee who does evaluation of property value

balance sheet -sheet of assets and liabilities

balloon payment - short term loan at a set percentage where the balance of the amount owed is due at the end of the loan or set time period

best efforts contracts - contract stating if best effort is made, there is no breach

bond - certificate proving debt

breach of contract - failure to perform conditions of a contract

broker - person who negotiates on your behalf

cancellation clause - ability to revoke a contract if what originally agreed upon was not performed

capital gains -profits realized when an asset is sold

capitalization - method of assessing the value of property to establish a fair estimate of net income

cede - to assign or grant, to give up

chain of title ownership - the successive change of legal ownership to property

closing price - the final price agreed upon

commercial - the use of real estate by business enterprises
contingency - possible outcome that depends on a future event

CPA - Certified Public Accountant

deed of trust -title to property used as security for a loan

default interest rate - increase in an interest rate when there is a failure to pay as promised

deferred maintenance - maintenance that is due but not yet performed

depreciation - reduction in value of property, also a fixed yearly deduction for tax purposes

due diligence -a legal standard, carefully making sure everything is in order

duplex - dwelling with two separate residences

earnest money - payment in part to bind a contract

easement - right of an owner to use the property of adjoining owner for a certain purpose

entity - a legal structure which is considered to have a real and separate existence

entrepreneur - one who assumes the risks of organizing a business and becoming a business owner

exemption -free from liability or government requirement

financials - accountings frequently used as proof of necessary funds to close a deal

foreclosure - when the rights in a mortgage are terminated and the property is put up for sale, normally for non payment of mortgage obligation

fourplex - dwelling with four separate residences

gains -increase in value

gross expenses - total of all expenses

gross lease - a lease which includes all operating costs

guarantor -one that guarantees payment of another's debt or obligation

habitability - capable of living in

impound account - money held in reserve

indemnify - agreement to secure another person or entity against loss

inspection report - inspector's report describing condition of property, usually done before purchase

liability insurance - insurance against specified risks

limited liability company - entity formed to limit liability and which is frequently taxed as a partnership

lien - legal claim on property to pay a debt

litigation - a lawsuit

losses - decrease in value

market value - the worth of property when compared to others that are similar on the market

median income - average income of the public

mediator - independent unbiased party that helps solve disputes

multi-family - property set up for more than one renter or family to occupy, such as a duplex or four plex

negative cash flow - paying out more than is coming in

operating statement - financial statement detailing operations

option fee - fee established for the right to exercise an option to buy at a certain price

performance contract - contract defining a promise to fulfill an obligation

promissory note - legal document that is a promise to meet agreed upon obligation

residential - property lived in for personal use

security deposit - money held by landlord to cover cleaning and other expenses if property is not kept in good condition by tenant

single-family home - occupied by one family

stock - certificate proving percentage ownership in a company

summary process - taking effect immediately and without delay instead of in the ordinary course of business

tax rolls - list of taxpayers responsible for taxes

tax shelter - protection from taxes that would have to be paid without the shelter

tenanted rental property - property rented by tenants

transactional attorney - attorney specializing in business and real estate transactions

undervaluation -an underestimation of the true value of a property

valuation - determining the worth of something

warranty - guarantee of performance

zoning - restrictions on property determined by governmental authorities

About the Author

Dr. Dolf de Roos began investing in real estate as an undergraduate student. Despite going on to earn a Ph.D. in electrical and electronic engineering from the University of Canterbury, Dolf increasingly focused on his flair for real estate investing, which has enabled him to have never had a job. He has, however, invested in many classes of real estate (residential, commercial, industrial, hospitality, and specialist) all over the world.

Today he is the chairman of the public company Property Ventures Limited, an innovative real estate investment company whose stated mission is to massively increase stockholders' worth. Over the years, Dolf was cajoled into sharing his investment strategies, and he has run seminars on the Psychology of Creating Wealth and on Real Estate Investing throughout North America, Australia, New Zealand, Asia, the Middle East, and Europe since the 1980s.

Beyond sharing his investment philosophy and strategies with tens of thousands of investors (beginners as well as seasoned experts), Dolf has also trained real estate agents, written and published numerous bestselling books on property, and introduced computer software designed to analyze and manage properties quickly and efficiently. He often speaks at investors' conferences, realtors' conventions, and his own international seminars, and regularly takes part in radio shows and television debates. Born in New Zealand, raised in Australia, New Zealand and Europe, Dolf, with six languages up his sleeve, offers a truly global perspective on the surprisingly lucrative wealth building opportunities of real estate. Dolf has shared the platform with his friend Robert Kiyosaki for many years and is one of his select Rich Dad's Advisors™.

To find out what you can learn from Dolf's willingness to share his knowledge about creating wealth through real estate, and to receive his free monthly newsletter, please visit his Web site at www.dolfderoos.com.

How to take advantage of resources available to create wealth though real estate

With real estate, as with most other activities in life, you cannot hope to learn all you need to know by reading one book once. Although real estate is far more stable, consistent, and dependable than many other financial activities, keeping up with trends and ahead of the competition is imperative. Read many books on the subject (the book you don't read cannot help you!), attend seminars, talk with other investors, and dream up your own ideas to try out in the market place.

Success leaves clues! We have a number of resources to help both aspiring and seasoned investors. Please visit our Web site www.dolfderoos.com to find out more about our: books, tapes, software, mentoring, seminar schedules, new products, services and events

Finally, remember that contrary to the saying knowledge is power, it is only applied knowledge that is power. It is not enough to know a lot about real estate - to achieve real estate riches, you must put the theories into action. It's the difference between being interested and being committed.

Subscribe to our Free Monthly Newsletter

We Trust that the resources available on our
Web site www.dolfderoos.com will empower you
and propel you on your way to not needing (or wanting!)
a job thanks to real estate.

About the Author

 Garrett Sutton, Esq., author of *Own Your Own Corporation, How to Buy and Sell a Business* and co-author of *Real Estate Loopholes,* all in the Rich Dad's Advisor series, is an attorney with over twenty years of experience in assisting individuals and businesses to determine their appropriate corporate structure, limit their liability, protect their assets, and advance their real estate, financial and personal goals.

Garrett and his law firm represent hundreds of corporations, limited liability companies, limited partnerships, and individuals in their real estate and business-related law matters, including incorporation, contracts, mergers and acquisitions, private and public company securities offerings, and ongoing business-related legal advice.

Garrett attended Colorado College and the University of California at Berkeley, where he received a B.S. in business administration in 1975. He graduated with a J.D. in 1978 from Hastings College of the Law, the University of California's law school in San Francisco. He is also a licensed real estate broker and real estate investor

Garrett is a member of the State Bar of Nevada, the State Bar of California, and the American Bar Association. He has written numerous professional articles and serves on the Publication Committee of the State Bar of Nevada.

Garrett enjoys speaking with entrepreneurs on the advantages of forming business entities. He is a frequent lecturer with Robert Kiyosaki's Rich Dad's Advisor team and with Success DNA.

He is also the founder of Success DNA, which assists entrepreneurs in achieving their goals. He is the author of *How to Use Limited Liability Companies and Limited Partnerships* in the Success DNA series, and writes for Success DNA's free newsletter, which is available at www.successdna.com. For more information on Garrett Sutton's law firm, please visit his website at www.sutlaw.com.

How Can I Protect My Real Estate Assets?

For more information on forming limited liability companies and limited partnerships to protect your real estate holdings in all 50 states, as well as useful tips and strategies, visit Nevada Corporate Centerís website at www.goconv.com or call toll free 1.877.683.9342.

Special Offer: Mention this book and receive a 5% discount on the basic formation fee.

Where Can I Receive More Free Entrepreneur Information?

Sign up to receive SuccessDNAís FREE e-newsletter featuring useful articles and entrepreneur resources. Visit www.successdna.com for more details.

Where Can I Find More Legal Information?

For further information about the author and his law firm, visit their site www.sutlaw.com, where you can review biographical notes, explanations of various practice areas and services offered by the firm, and how to contact the firm for more information about initial consultation arrangements and engagement of the firm for an array of legal services.

SUTTON LAWRENCE,LLP
ATTORNEYS AT LAW

SuccessDNA Publications
Order Here to Receive Our Quality Business and Financial Books

The Success DNA Guide to Real Estate Investment and Management, written by Dolf de Roos, Ph.D. and Garrett Sutton, Esq., offers practical information on the essential elements of real estate acquisition and ownership.

How to Use Limited Liability Companies & Limited Partnerships, written by Garrett Sutton, Esq. This publication is an in-depth study of how the special characteristics of limited liability partnerships and limited liability may be used to your advantage for asset protection and wealth management.

Easy Accounting for Real Estate Investors, written by Diane Kennedy, CPA. The must have guide for recordkeeping and accounting requirements for real estate owners.

The Healthy Executive, written by Amy Sutton, is a complete explanation and method for attaining and maintaining your most important asset, your physical health. Topics from diet to exercise are presented in an easy to read and practical manner.

❑ Yes, please send me:

___copies of *The Success DNA Guide to Real Estate Investment and Management* at $17.95 each
___copies of *How to Use Limited Liability Companies and Limited Partnerships* at $19.95 each
___copies of *Easy Accounting for Real Estate Investors* at $24.95 each
___copies of *The Healthy Executive* at $19.95 each

Please add $6.95 shipping and handling per book (NV residents please add $1.70 sales tax per book). Canadian orders must be accompanied by a postal money order in U.S. funds. Allow 15 days for delivery.

My check or money order for $_____is enclosed.

Please charge my: ❑[VISA] ❑[MASTERCARD] ❑[AMERICAN EXPRESS]
Name:_____
Address:_____
City/State/Zip:_____
Phone:_____Email:_____
Card #_____Exp. Date:_____
Signature:_____

Please make your check or money order payable and return to:
SuccessDNA Inc.* P.O. Box 1450 * Verdi, NV 89439
Call your credit card order to: 1-800-293-7411 or fax to (775) 824-0105
Also visit www.successdna.com to order books or to sign up for our newsletter!